PRAISE FOR *THE 30-SECOND GOLF SWING*

"T. J. Tomasi is one of the brightest instructors we've ever worked with at *GOLF Magazine*. He has an unquenchable thirst for golf knowledge and in *The 30-Second Golf Swing*, he dives deep into the last frontier of golf performance—the role of the brain in shooting lower scores. Tomasi delves inside the intellectual and emotional nuances that affect performance. If you play to win, this is a must read."

—Lorin Anderson, managing editor for instruction, *GOLF Magazine*

"The tour players I coach understand that an important part of becoming a champion is implementing the concepts and techniques outlined in this book. *The 30-Second Golf Swing* is one of the most outstanding books on golf available today and I feel strongly that the guidance provided by T. J. Tomasi will provide a key missing ingredient to improving your own golf game."

—Mike McGetrick, 1999 National PGA Teacher of the Year

"*The 30-Second Golf Swing* addresses a part of golf so often neglected—the mental aspects of playing. As I read, I could picture all of the things people do wrong and remember doing them myself. T. J. Tomasi easily guided my thinking toward the positive and the self-assured and helped me notice the negative and destructive thoughts. I have been looking for the Go signals and beginning to recognize the No signals before hitting a shot that has little chance of being on target. It feels right and with each Go signal and successful shot confidence grows. It is not hard to see why Dr. Tomasi is one of golf's great teachers."

—Ken Graap, 4 handicap, president of Virtually Better Inc.

Also by T. J. Tomasi

How to Break 90 *with Mike Adams*
The Little Book of Putting
Total Golf *with Mike Adams*
The LAWS of the Golf Swing *with Mike Adams*
Break 100 Now *with Mike Adams*
Never Out of the Hole *with Mike Adams*
Play Better Golf for Seniors *with Mike Adams*
Play Better Golf for Women *with Kathryn Maloney and Mike Adams*
Play Golf for Juniors *with Mike Adams*
Play Better Golf *with Mike Adams*

THE 30-SECOND
GOLF SWING

HOW TO TRAIN YOUR BRAIN TO IMPROVE YOUR GAME

T. J. Tomasi, Ph.D.
PGA Professional

with Kathryn Maloney

A MOUNTAIN LION BOOK

Quill

A HarperResource Book
An Imprint of HarperCollins*Publishers*

HarperCollins books may be purchased for educational, business,
or sales promotional use. For information please write:
Special Markets Department, HarperCollins Publishers Inc.,
10 East 53rd Street, New York, NY 10022.

First HarperResource/Quill paperback edition published 2003

Designed by Oksana Kushnir

Illustrations by Folio Graphics

The Library of Congress has catalogued the hardcover edition as follows:
Tomasi, T. J.
    The 30-Second Golf Swing : how to train your brain to improve your
game / T. J. Tomasi with Kathryn Maloney.—1st ed.
        p.   cm.
    Includes index.
    ISBN 0-06-019610-6
    1. Golf (instruction)   2. Golf—Psychological aspects.   I. Title: 30-
second golf swing.   II. Maloney, Kathryn.   III. Title.
GV979.S9 T56   2001
796.352'3—dc21   00-047290

ISBN 0-06-052020-5 (pbk.)
    03   04   05   06   07   RRD   10   9   8   7   6   5   4   3   2   1

In 1993, I wrote the foreword to Chuck Hogan's book, *Learning Golf*. At that time, I called him an iconoclast who had forged a new road in golf instruction and this is even more true today as he spends most of his time exploring the reasons why one athlete excels and another, technically equal, does not. He and his wife, Shelly, have produced a video called *Golf and the Intelligence of Play* that identifies and describes the conditions necessary for great play. You will find the origins of excellence, the role of deep play, the Zone, the need for psychological and emotional safety, and all the other elements that constitute the magical environment necessary for success.

Chuck Hogan is one of the most successful coaches to the Tour professionals. His client list reads like a Who's Who of top money winners: Peter Jacobsen, Colleen Walker, John Cook, Johnny Miller, Raymond Floyd, Grant Waite, Duffy Waldorf, Cindy Rarick, D. A. Weibring, and many others.

But he deals with "regular" students too and he has always taught us to question the established beliefs not just about golf but about life in general. When you say to Chuck, "I don't understand," he says, "Good, that's a start." For Hogan, only the smug claim certainty and only the foolish demand perfect clarity. You don't have an experience with Chuck Hogan—he *is* the experience.

There is no question in my mind that this book would not exist without the genius of Chuck Hogan. He was the first to promote many of the ideas in this book as they relate to golf, and the interaction we have had over the years has provided the platform that supports my own ideas about golf and how to run your brain.

Thank you, Chuck.
T. J. Tomasi
July 19, 2000

The mailing address to reach Chuck Hogan is:

Athletics and the Intelligence of Play Foundation, Inc.
1915 Jackpine Place
Redmond, Oregon 97756

http://www.magicalathlete.com/donations.html
toll free 1-877-529-7529

CONTENTS

There has never been a golfer who had a mind like Nicklaus. I saw guys who hit the ball a lot better than Nicklaus, but it's not the striking of the ball that makes the difference.

—GARY PLAYER

There are no swing mechanics in this book; no tips on posture, zero on how you should hold the club in your hands, precious little about your balance, and absolutely nothing about how to cure a hook or slice. To be sure, swing mechanics are so important they cannot be overlooked if you want to be a good golfer, so I have recorded my opinions on them in other books, most notably, *The LAWS of the Golf Swing*. But while an effective golf swing is an essential ingredient to compete at the game's highest level, it is far from the only ingredient necessary to be a champion. As Raymond Floyd said, "If a great golf swing put you high on the money list, there'd be some of us who would be broke."

The same is true at almost every level of amateur and professional golf. Playing to your potential involves far more than the one and a half seconds you spend swinging the club. The golf swing then is only one piece in the pattern of great golf, a pattern for running your brain that I call the 30-Second Swing. Thirty seconds, give or take a few, is how long it takes to plan, evaluate, and execute every shot. In order to give yourself your best chance of success you must learn to apply all your resources to each and every shot you hit, both in practice and in play. By doing this, you can impose your will on the golf course so that you subject all of the stimuli coming at you to a rigorous organization. Whether it's the pressure of a tough shot, the jiggling coins in the pocket of a competitor, the change in the wind after you've chosen your club, the beverage cart bearing down on you as you are about to hit—these stimuli are under control once you know how to use the 30-Second Swing.

Granted, these techniques for managing your brain are not magic bullets that will turn you into a Tour player in your spare time, but if you use them while you play, you can take a giant step along the road to self-mastery. You'll have a full understanding of what goes wrong on the golf course and you'll learn to play at the highest level possible given your talent for the game.

You'll learn how to recognize what's happening to you when your game starts to slip and you'll have tactics that allow you to regain control. Most golfers recognize the importance of the mental or inner game, as it is often called, but without well-defined, concrete strategies and techniques, you're no better off with a brain full of mental game stuff than one full of swing thoughts.

F. Scott Fitzgerald said that the rich are different, and in golf the champions are different. There is something more than just a golf swing that separates a champion from the rest of the pack. Champions possess an arsenal of techniques that allow them full access to the motor program that runs their golf swing. Average golfers, even if they have a decent swing, often lose access to it as soon as they step onto the golf course.

A RELATIVE CHAMPION

Throughout this book you'll read words like *champion* and *great player*, but the references aren't limited to players the caliber of a Jack Nicklaus or a Ben Hogan, a Karrie Webb or a Tiger Woods. A champion is a golfer who can play his or her best golf when it matters the most, be it for a five-dollar Nassau, a club championship, or a national championship. The goal of this book is to make your scores match your talent for the game. You'll learn how to train your brain to run your game so that you develop a mastery, not of golf—that would be presumptuous—but of yourself.

A POINT OF CLARIFICATION

Training and then running your brain correctly—controlling your thoughts, reactions, memories, and images—is essential to playing the game to your potential. Once you learn golf's mechanical elements, running your brain is the only element left to control.

In reference to the brain, though, it is important to remember that much of its workings remains a mystery. The brain is by far the most complicated organ and, to a large degree, an intricacy that awaits unraveling. Part of the complexity comes from what may be the ultimate paradox: the instrument we use to study the brain is the brain itself, which is like a thermometer trying to learn all there is to know about temperature.

Though no one knows exactly how the brain works, it doesn't mean that we must remain silent on its importance. Nor does it mean that we can't recognize and describe a brain that is operating properly when it comes to golf. In this regard I often resort to heuristic models that, although they may not be entirely accurate, are image-rich and close enough to what's real to get our arms around some rather slippery concepts.

For example, while the idea that every detail of your golf

swing is precisely encoded in a perfect neural map is inviting, it is probably not the case. When you decide to make a golf swing, there is a motor program for it in your brain. Instead of issuing exact instructions to the muscles that are not to be deviated from, the brain issues advice or suggestions as to how to get the job done. This makes sense since important local conditions, say in your shoulder or hip joint, may not be available to the higher brain centers in time to make key adjustments. In terms of survival, this is a clever bit of flexibility that is built in. If you only know how to move your shoulder in one or two ways, you would be unable to defend yourself when the tiger leaps from a new direction, or when a sudden load is exerted on a joint.

A motor control system that depended on a centralized command structure would not be the most effective way of surviving under varying conditions, so it is of the utmost survival value to preserve some autonomy at the local level. Research scientist John Annett of the University of Warwick in England explains the concept as follows.

"Although absolute values of felt force, distance and direction can be retained with moderate accuracy for short periods it is unlikely that we rely on simple sensory-motor memory of discrete movements to remember how to perform skilled motor tasks. The world in which we live and the actions we have to take are far too variable for it to be worthwhile to memorize precise movement. It is rather through a set of outline plans . . . abstractly defined, that we are able to remember how to solve familiar motor problems."

This autonomy at the level of physical execution is one reason a golf swing will never have perfect consistency and any player who has this goal is doomed to frustration. Because of the design of the golfer, golf is a game of misses, and the player with the best misses wins. Nature cares only for survival and not one whit for our golf games. Knowing this makes our failures more bearable.

CHAPTER 1

Training Your Brain

CHAMPIONS CONTROL THEIR GAME by funneling their golf experience through a process that I call the 30-Second Swing, which brings sequence and order to their golf game. You have the same type of filter available to you. You can exercise this control over both your external and internal flow of experience, a control that will allow you to take a big step up on the performance curve. It might not make you a champion at the highest level—there is the matter of talent—but adopting the 30-Second Swing will train your brain to run your game so that you can play to your talent level.

The 30-second time frame is only an approximation; each player has to refine the pattern and customize it to his or her personality. But the insights and techniques, once mastered, will enable you to play to your potential. You'll be a champion in your own right with your brain trained to play golf instead of golf swing.

WHEN THE WHEELS FALL OFF

It's a relatively harmless par-5 with a green you can miss 40 yards to the right and still be okay, yet our spotlight player pulls his second shot way left into the jailhouse woods. Or how about the huge green big enough to hold a 747? From 80 yards away, this same player buries a ball in the lip of the bunker.

These aren't snapshots from a Saturday morning best ball or local club championship. They're mistakes made by Greg Norman, at the time one of the world's best golfers. The first mistake occurred on the 8th hole of the 1996 Masters, the initial step en route to one of the most astonishing collapses in modern golf competition. The second mistake took place several years earlier on his way to erasing another substantial lead on the back nine of the Tournament Players Championship.

Scott Hoch, no stranger to a breakdown now and then, commented on Norman's disintegration over the last eleven holes at the '96 Masters. "You get on a train like that and it's hard to get off. I didn't expect it. He's proven himself to be mentally tough."

FAMOUS COME-FROM-AHEAD LOSSES

Norman is not the first to have been playing at a gallop and suddenly thrown a shoe. Arnold Palmer lost the 1966 U.S. Open in a playoff after leading Billy Casper by seven shots with eight holes to play. Ed Snead lost the 1979 Masters after leading by five with eighteen holes to play. Six-time PGA Tour Player of the Year Tom Watson, ahead after three rounds, shot 80 to lose the 1978 PGA Championship. And back in 1919, unknown Mike Brady shot an 80 to lose the U.S. Open after holding the fifty-four-hole lead.

So what happens when the wheels fall off? How does a golfer

beat the course into submission with a 63 on Thursday and limp home with a 78 on Sunday? Whatever it is, it must be powerful stuff—much more powerful than just the swing. What, exactly, does a golfer lose control of?

I suggest it's the mental side that goes first, followed shortly thereafter by the swing itself. But since the physical swing is so visually apparent, we blame it for the collapse, rather than the thought patterns hidden from our view. The problem with attaching so much importance to the swing is that it leads to a vicious cycle that can last the rest of your golfing life. Most golfers labor under the basic misconception that swing mechanics are the only things that are important in sending the ball to target—if only you could get that right, you could be a player.

Using this logic, a good shot means you made a good swing; a bad shot means you made a bad swing. Therefore, when you hit bad shots, you're not ready to play golf until you fix the bad swing, so it's off to the range. This destructive reasoning traps you in a break-it-fix-it-break-it-fix-it cycle. Since you think your swing is always the culprit, swing mechanics so consume your focus, there is no time or energy left to play the target game called golf. On the course you may appear to be playing golf, but you're really playing "break it, fix it." As golf professional and mental game guru Chuck Hogan has pointed out, many golfers unwittingly spend their entire lives in this remedial loop.

In 1998, an obscure teaching pro led the PGA Tour's Honda Classic heading into the last nine holes on Sunday. He was playing beautifully when, out of nowhere, he topped a two-iron from the middle of the 15th fairway and proceeded to fall apart on the final three holes. Did his swing suddenly let him down? He had probably hit thousands of perfect two-irons on the practice tee with "his" swing, so it wasn't a sudden malfunction in the motor program called "golf swing for hitting with the two-iron." The problem was that he didn't have access to that motor program because of the pressure. His perception of the situation blocked his access to his swing. He didn't need more swing training; he needed more brain training.

TRAIN YOUR BRAIN TO RUN YOUR GAME

Training your brain to run your game is the central theme of this book. Champions can't control *what* is happening to them, but they can control *how* they respond to what is happening to them. Their thought process is of the highest quality because they have trained their brain as diligently as they have trained their swing. You can call it knowing how to win, mental toughness, golf smarts, paying your dues, or simply experience, but whatever you call it, a trained brain is the sine qua non of a champion.

Of course, not every golfer has the combination of trained brain and trained swing working for them. There are three possible combinations:

1. An untrained swing combined with a trained brain produces tenacious players who get the most out of their swing. These golfers have much potential because once they improve their swing mechanics (a relatively easy feat), they will have a trained brain to run the show.

2. The majority of amateurs suffer double jeopardy: neither their swing nor their brains are well trained for golf. In addition to training their brain, they need the help of an expert teacher and some time on the range.

3. The third combination is a player with a sound golf swing and an untrained golf brain. When this player's swing goes, the game goes with it. These are fragile players, especially when it

comes to sustained performance. They are often considered underachievers or chokers. They put most of their energy into developing a driving range swing that can't save them when things take a turn for the worse—as they tend to do on a golf course. They can play along quite well for a few holes and suddenly— poof—it's gone. A bad bounce, a hole-out by their opponent from the bunker, a missed two-footer, a myriad surprises and stresses can send them spiraling out of control. Then, of course, it's back to the range for more swing repair.

"THINKERING"

Golfers who have failed to train their brain can easily become victims of "Thinkering," a combination of thinking about and then tinkering with their golf swing. Thinkering is a bad habit that those who have trained their brain don't have.

Now it is true that some players, although they were already champions, set about to improve by making major swing changes. For example, in 1979, Jack Nicklaus made such a change when he realized that he needed to shallow his swing plane to play better in the wind. Nick Faldo underwent a complete swing over-haul, as did Nick Price and Mark O'Meara. And Tiger Woods, after winning the 1997 Masters by twelve shots with an 18-under-par tournament record, spent over a year working on a new and much improved swing.

But these are not examples of Thinkering. These changes were not knee-jerk reactions to a few bad shots. These champi-ons planned their swing changes after thoughtful, in-depth analysis of their game and their goals. They created a step-by-step blueprint for change, and those changes occurred under the watchful eye of an expert instructor. They accepted that their performance would suffer during the learning process and they were prepared to pay the price. Most important, all these players were fully committed to their changes and gave the learning process enough time for their brains to be completely retrained.

A WELL-TRAINED BRAIN IN ACTION
Nick Price arrived at the 1994 British Open having won the last event he played in and was, by his own assessment, "hitting the ball better than I ever had before." As the practice rounds began on Monday at Turnberry, his swing inexplicably vanished. "The experienced player does not panic in this situation," Price explained. "I knew that the swing changes I had made were correct. I was having trouble simply because of human nature. There was no reason to shift focus from what I had been working on to something new. I firmly believed that eventually my body would adjust to the cooler conditions in Scotland and also to the time change. The swing was still there. I just had to trust it." Price knew his swing was still "in there" and it was this confidence that allowed his swing to return in time for Price to win the Claret Jug.

In the next chapter, you'll see that when champions practice to keep their swing in good working order, they aren't Thinkering. They have a Strength and Weakness Profile that they are constantly evaluating and updating, and their practice goal is to keep their strengths current and to convert their weaknesses to strengths. To play like a champion there must be a point when, except for strength and weakness upgrades, you are done with your swing mechanics.

HOW CHAMPIONS PLAY

You won't see the headline "Tiger Woods Forgets Swing—Misses Cut." But if headline writers understood how the brain stores, categorizes, and retrieves the images it needs to play great golf, you might see "Woods Not Running Brain Well—Misses Cut." How champions perform has less to do with the golf swing, and much to do with how well they run their thoughts, emotions, and reactions.

YOU DON'T FORGET YOUR SWING

Once you learn your swing, it's in your brain for good. Unless there is a brain injury, it's in there and you won't lose it, as in, An hour ago I had my wallet and now it's gone forever 'cause I left it on the airplane.

Studies in motor learning show that once a skill is learned it is never forgotten. Furthermore, after a year without practice, the performance level returns to 80 percent after ten days of retraining. So your swing is in there all right, just like other motor skills such as shoe tying, bike riding, running, and swimming. You cannot forget them because they're captured in neural networks. Rather than thinking in terms of forgetting how to swing, I suggest that there are circumstances that deny you full access to the motor program called your golf swing. Your "A Swing"—the one that fires on all cylinders when your game is under control—is temporarily unavailable.

One such example occurred in the 1999 PGA Grand Slam: Davis Love played nearly perfect golf the first day to crush José Maria Olazabal 6 and 5. Twenty-four hours later, playing against the imposing Tiger Woods, Love went from shooting a seven-under 29 on the front nine against Olazabal to a one-over 37 against Woods. In his match against Olazabal, Davis Love was obviously running his own brain with perfect access to his motor program called golf. In the second match, Tiger Woods was running Love's brain and access was denied. Love said, "He got 1-up on an eagle and when he gets off like that, he's hard to beat . . . I could feel the door closing." And this was only the 2nd hole!

So even the great players have lapses in their ability to run their brain effectively, but these are rare. Most of the time golf's elite play the game in a way that is foreign to the majority of golfers. How does a champion play the game? Let's first examine what they don't do.

CHAMPIONS DON'T PLAY BY DON'TS

Don't hit it left. . . .

Don't hit it in the water. . . .

Playing by don'ts won't get the job done. This golfer's brain is muddled with the fuzzy set of instructions to don't-*do*-something. The problem is, in its initial processing, your brain doesn't consider the don't in the statement, "Don't hit it fat." As Chuck Hogan showed so well in his video entitled *Nice Shot,* the actual message your brain receives is driven by the image on your mental screen: hit it fat. And, being a perfect learner, you do exactly that.

Humans are image makers, and images form the blueprints for our behavior. If you need proof, close your eyes and focus on your mental screen. Now tell yourself, "Don't think about the Statue of Liberty." What popped up on the screen was, of course, the very image you ordered yourself not to think about. Your mind has a mind of its own.

So when you tell yourself, "Don't hit it in the water," your brain first considers the topic in image form. You see, feel, and hear yourself hitting the ball in the water. Now all that is necessary to complete this bad shot is to translate the image into behavior. A second or two later you're wet, and probably angry. It's no consolation that you just gave a clinic on how to hit it into the water—you did it perfectly, albeit perfectly wrong.

Was your swing at fault? No, your swing was the instrument, but failure to run your brain correctly was the root cause. A well-trained brain does not play by don'ts.

Dan Foresman prepared for the Masters one year by repeatedly watching a section of Jack Nicklaus's video, *Golf's Eighteen Greatest Holes,* which dealt with the pivotal par-3 12th at Augusta National. One segment showed Sandy Lyle hitting two balls in the water on number 12. Like the perfect learner we all are, Foresman arrived at the 12th on the last day of the tournament and put two balls in the water.

CHAMPIONS DON'T PLAY BY DO'S

Keep the right arm tucked. . . .

Stay down. . . .

Drop the club into the slot. . . .

You create mental images as you process information about your world. These images then cue your physical responses. When you're late, you run after a taxi; when you're scared, you run away from the tiger. How your muscles get the job done—the technique of running—is accomplished with unconscious competence. You don't have to think about the how-to of the physical response as you do it. If you did, chances are you'd miss the taxi, or be eaten by the tiger!

When you swing a golf club, though, the urge to think-while-doing is very strong. This puts your conscious mind in control and, in the moment it takes to complete your swing, you don't have time for conscious in-swing instructions. As Ben Hogan said, "The downswing is no place to give yourself a lesson." If you're still calculating what to do while you're doing it, you dramatically reduce your chances of making a good swing. This is why playing by do's doesn't work. Do's introduce a conscious element into what should be unconscious execution.

Ralph Guldahl was asked to write an instruction book after he won the 1937 and 1938 U.S. Open. He analyzed his golf swing in such detail that he ruined his game. After he figured out exactly what he did, he couldn't do it anymore. A well-trained brain does not play by do's. If you use the do-do system that's how you'll play—like a dodo!

TARGETING

So if champions don't play by don'ts, and they don't play by do's, how do they play? Champions, at every level, play by targeting. Every shot is a target-player interaction where the player connects to the target through the senses, making the connection a multisensorial experience. When you're plugged into the target, your senses trigger feelings, visual images, rhythms, cadences, and so forth that are translated automatically into motor responses. In other words, based on your perception of the target, your body moves to create the correct distance and direction for the shot.

> Terry Larson, a speed golfer, knows how to get out of his own way. He shot 75 playing eighteen holes in just under forty minutes. The day before Larson spent three and a half hours touring the same course in 77 strokes. He offered this explanation: "When you play sports like baseball or tennis you react to the target. In golf, the ball just sits there and you can end up thinking too much. In speed golf you run up to the ball, find the target and hit it."

CHAMPIONS HAVE A DIFFERENT VIEW: THE SWING IS *NOT* THE ONLY THING

As I said in the introduction, there's more to great golf than the one and a half seconds spent swinging the club, though it is often the sole focus for the majority of amateurs who play the game. To a champion, the golf swing is only a piece in a much larger pattern of playing the game. The pattern includes handling not only external experiences (like noise, wind, what your opponent is doing) but also internal experiences that manifest themselves as feelings, emotions, and internal self-talk—the currency that makes up the inner content of your brain.

CHAMPIONS CONTROL SELF-TALK

Internal chatter, at loud levels, is not conducive to good golf. Most golfers have a habit of talking to themselves, and you had better be careful what you say—you may be listening.

There are three kinds of self-talk:

1. Posi-talk: You're the spin doctor and you have the ability to put a positive interpretation on events and outcomes. The glass is half full, the wind is your friend, bad bounces are part of the game; unfair courses, rules, etc., are the same for everyone. These kinds of expressions are the staples of posi-talk.

There are many self-help experts who sing the praises of positive thinking and nurturing affirmations such as "Every day, in every way, I'm getting better and better" or "I'm supergreat and getting better." Emile Coué founded a school of psychotherapy based on the principle that if you repeat an affirmation enough, and the affirmation is possible, the brain converts belief into the physical reality. It's no secret that positive autosuggestion is a powerful tool, and you'll rarely hear anyone condemn its use.

2. Prophylactic-talk: Though it sounds like nega-talk, it doesn't have the self-critical element and, therefore, it protects your self-image and can actually be a good strategy. Prophylactic-talk protects your self-image by placing the blame for failure on outside agencies not under your control. Poor putting is caused by awful greens, bad play is caused by the weather, the noise, the architect; you're playing too little or too much . . . it's always something or someone else's fault.

If used appropriately, this type of talk insulates you from the consequences of personal failure so that your self-image doesn't take direct hits. Problems arise, however, if you take this strategy to an extreme and use excuses to mask your inadequacies. For example, the fastest way to lose your putting stroke is to miss a few easy putts and lose your confidence. If you're a good putter, you can retain your confidence when you have an off day—and live to putt well another day—if you blame your failure on the poor condition of the greens.

But be careful. Attributing missed putts to bad greens only works if your putting stroke is solid. If you always putt badly and, rather than addressing the problem, you blame it on the greens, and never work on your stroke, then you'll never learn to putt well.

Golf writer Lorne Rubenstein's description of Jack Nicklaus shows how the greatest of golfers used prophylactic-talk to his advantage.

"He's been called Carnac after the Johnny Carson character who thought he knew everything," writes Rubenstein. "He's rarely hit a bad shot because there's always been something to blame—the glint of the sun on his putter blade, the wind coming up at the top of his swing, a soft spot on a green from which the ball didn't release. These . . . are symbolic of his strong sense of self-belief, and they are part of the reason he has won 20 major championships. You know the man of whom I am speaking, one Jack William Nicklaus."

3. Nega-talk: A condescending, destructive, critical, glass-is-half-empty type of talk in which you berate yourself, call yourself names, and do yourself absolutely no good. Using nega-talk, you speak to yourself in ways that you would not accept from other people. This habit destroys your self-confidence and lays Tracks of Failure in your brain because its tone and content label your experience as negative. Nega-talk ranges from verbal assaults at high volume to subtle slights and diamond-hard digs that find their mark. After all, who knows better than you where your self-image soft spots are?

The volume, rhythm, and tone are as important as the words you choose to trash yourself. There is sarcastic nega-talk: "Nice going, Mr. Choke." There are the rapid-fire, staccato barbs that castigate your self-image: "I'm the worst golfer on the planet." And there are simple sentences of resignation delivered with a convincing matter-of-factness: "I'm not cut out to be a golfer, I'll never learn this game, I'm just not athletic enough to play golf."

BANISH THE NEGA-TALK

Of the three, nega-talk must be banished from your self-talk repertoire for two reasons. First, it's a negative anchor that lays down Tracks of Failure, harmful resources that poison your brain. Second, nega-talk convinces your brain that the body is under attack, the first step to being flooded with antigolf chemicals via the fight/flight response. Thus, an important tool in playing your best golf is to monitor your brand of self-talk and eliminate or, at very least, modify your nega-talk.

For example, when you catch yourself in nega-talk, change the way you do it. Lower the volume, slow it down, use a Southern drawl, a clipped British accent, or make your internal voice a Rodney Dangerfield imitation. Make the voice say please and thank you. Soon, your nega-talk will become so ridiculous that it will be a source of humor. Once you can do that, it's no longer a threat, no matter what the content.

Nega-talk produces self-fulfilling prophecies that result in a series of perfect permissions to fail. If you believe that positive autosuggestion works, so then must negative autosuggestion. If you want to play your best golf, you need to stop the nega-talk.

STICKS, STONES, AND WORDS TOO

Contrary to popular belief, it appears that words, not just sticks and stones, can and do cause harm. Researchers report that words with negative connotations about aging can have negative effects on seniors' cardiovascular health, such as driving up blood pressure. But there is also some good news. Positive words about aging helped to reduce blood pressure in a group of seniors.

Reporting in the July 2000 issue of the *Journal of Gerontology*, Dr. Becca Levy of the Yale University School of Medicine in New Haven, Connecticut, and colleagues write that their "research presents for the first time the effect of self-stereotypes of aging on a physiological process: the cardiovascular response to stress." Levy told Reuters Health that "exposing older individuals to negative stereotypes of aging [increased] the participants' . . . blood pressure significantly . . . [suggesting] that the negative beliefs or stereotypes about aging that many older individuals encounter in their daily lives may increase their cardiovascular stress."

The Journal of Gerontology

THREE BASIC MODES

There are three basic modes the human brain creates: Analytical, physical, and emotional. As you move through the 30-

Second Swing, you'll need to be in the right mode at the right time. If not, you'll be mismoded, a condition that disconnects you from your target and ruins your game.

Analytical: The analytical mode is a state where you consider events logically and determine solutions rationally. You're detached and methodical, an ideal mode for solving a puzzle or deciding how to get your golf ball from point A to point B. It's your data-gathering mode where your senses are wide open. In this mode you make your plan and develop your maps of the territory.

Physical: When you're in your physical mode you're performing an action such as swinging your golf club. This is your doing mode where your muscles are responding to the plan absent any interference from conscious instructions.

Emotional: The emotional mode is the third, your feeling mode. This is your interactive state where you mark events with emotive responses that not only make you feel good or bad, mad or sad, but also lay the groundwork for memories that will influence your future behavior.

LIFE IS ONE BIG MODE SWITCH

Life, it seems, is never on an even keel. A wise man once said, "You can never put your foot in the same river twice." Another wise man phrased it a bit differently: "You can't go home again." Life is all about change, a seamless flow of experience, where you switch from mode to mode as the situation warrants—switches that for the most part you don't even realize you've made.

One of the things that makes a movie or book great is that the writer or director drops you into the flow by knowing how to take you from mode to mode, putting you into the right mode at exactly the right time. When fantasy has the flow of life, it takes on the feel of life and thereby seems real.

So, when the hero is fighting the villain, you're shifting in your seat, wincing when he takes one on the chin, ducking as the knife whizzes by his ear. You're actually there in your physical mode, completely involved in the action. Then, when the heroine is in her emotional mode, you're in the emotional mode with her. Empathetic if she's sad, and right by her side endorsing her demands for vengeance on the villain because he killed her lover! Then, when you are trying to figure out what the murderer's next move will be, you're just where you should be, in your analytical mode, thinking, "What if he does this?" or "Suppose she does that."

WATCHING THE WATCH

The problem is that if you're in one mode when you're supposed to be in another, the flow is broken and the experience no longer seems authentic. I remember as a teenager watching a Hollywood movie about ancient Egypt that was so realistic—complete with pharaohs, pyramids, and the sprawling desert—that I was enthralled. Then somewhere in the middle of the movie, I spotted one of the extras wearing a wristwatch. For the rest of the movie, I couldn't resist checking the wrist of every character on the screen. The director had lost me; I was mismoded. And, if you're not careful, it's easy to be mismoded when you play golf.

GOING APE FOR GOLF

As you'll see, the flow of mode states has a basic sequence in golf that I call APE, an acronym for analytical, physical, and emotional. Great players have learned to be in the right mode at the right time and, when they are playing well, they are never mode-stuck. Mode switches are pivotal. You should not be in your emotional mode when you're trying to figure out what shot to play. If you're still upset about a putt you missed on the last green when it comes time to plan your next tee shot, you have a problem.

You need to control your modes by knowing what mode you should be in, and flowing from one mode to another at the appropriate time. This is why the 30-Second Swing is so efficacious: it allows you to switch modes automatically.

GOLF MODES

In the analytical mode you're locating the target and developing the plan to get there. You're relying on your senses and knowledge to plot the exact relationship between you and your target. Next, in your physical mode, you're creating the body motion necessary to get the ball to the target. The third part of the sequence is the emotional response to the outcome. After the physical execution, you analyze your result, mark it with the appropriate emotion, and then prepare for the next shot. Thus, the tie between you and the target ends the moment you face a new target. You must be agile enough to leave one target-player loop and enter another, turning your full attention to the new target. Each relationship is full, running the gamut from analytic to emotional, always in order and never stuck in any one mode.

TRAINING YOUR BRAIN: THE 30-SECOND SWING SUMMARY

The pattern that can make all this happen is the 30-Second Swing, the outline of which is presented below.

PLAN. The pattern begins to take form as you stand behind the ball, in your analytical mode. You'll gather information about the target and process it into a plan that will best meet your goal of hitting the ball to the target.

You'll formulate your plan with consideration to your Strength and Weakness Profile, the circumstances (match play or medal, one-up or two-down, etc.), and the conditions of play (lie, wind, hazards, etc.) and then choose the correct club. Your plan should match your Strength and Weakness Profile perfectly so that you receive permission from your subconscious mind to play the shot with confidence. This congruence between your plan and your capabilities expresses itself as a Go signal.

RELAX. The relaxation response is a scientifically verified bodily process that, when implemented, will allow you to take control of your stress level. You'll learn how to summon the relaxation response so you can fully image, without distraction, the shot that will fulfill your plan.

IMAGE. Images cue motor behavior, and they are powerful tools used by champions in all occupations. The past is relived through imagery; the present is portrayed by it, and the future is conceptualized in imagery. The power to produce vibrant multi-sensorial images before, during, and after each golf shot is a key to golf excellence. Though imagery is a natural function of your brain, most golfers don't use this power source to good advantage. Their images are either weak, lifeless representations with limited effectiveness or strong and compelling images of failure.

THE REHEARSAL. The practice swing is a kinesthetic cue that can serve as a perfect rehearsal for your actual swing. It is a lost art among amateurs, and one of the most misunderstood elements in the 30-Second Swing's pattern. You can only make an effective practice swing with full attention to, and full intention of, creating an exact rehearsal of a real swing. This is where you program in your swing key or guiding thought.

The successful completion of your rehearsal signals your full commitment to your plan and acts as a transition to your physical mode. From here, an avalanche of Go signals begins.

FINAL COMMITMENT. The Commitment Line is a clear demarcation between full endorsement of your plan and a series of temporary commitments, each modified or discarded as new information is brought to bear. Stepping across the Commitment Line means there is nothing else to consider and you are fully devoted to your plan. If, after crossing the Commitment Line, new information causes the need for a new plan (a No signal), then you step back behind the Commitment Line and run the pattern again to reestablish your commitment.

AIM THEN ALIGN. When you reach the ball, first aim your club face where you want the ball to start, then align your body to your club face. This takes care of the direction requirement, leaving you free to focus on creating the correct distance, a task essentially completed when you select the right club.

DISTANCE FIX. Though you fulfill the distance requirement for your shot by choosing the correct club, one last look at your target validates your plan. You lock on the target and ready yourself to pull the trigger.

REIMAGE. This is an expanded and more complete representation of the initial image included in the final commitment. The target is displayed on your mental screen using the technique called Image Retention Ability (IRA), a skill necessary in a sport where you don't look at the target while you swing.

FINAL GO SIGNAL. A confirmation of your initial Go signal.

PHYSICAL SWING. Guided by imagery and fueled by the Go signal, the swing itself is a freewheeling, nonmanipulated physical act that relies on the principles of physics.

THE EVALUATION PHASE. The part of your 30-Second Swing where outcomes are evaluated, marked, and then stored as part of an ever-expanding database that is the source of your up-to-date Strength and Weakness Profile.

ANCHORING. The process of marking and embedding experience in the neural networks by using emotions. The more you emotionalize an event, the more influential it becomes in effecting subsequent similar behavior in similar circumstances. The anchoring technique involves emotionalizing and storing good golf experiences and dissociating from bad golf experiences so they will not be saved as deep Tracks of Failure.

TRACKS OF EXCELLENCE. Using the anchoring technique, neural networks that contain positive golf experience are stored in the brain. The goal is to create as many Tracks of Excellence as you can and to limit the production of Tracks of Failure. A golfing database filled with Tracks of Failure severely limits your ability to play your best golf. Although you still may become a very good player, you will never achieve your talent potential unless you fill your brain with Tracks of Excellence.

SUMMARY

Watch any good player and you'll see a consistent playing pattern. Unfortunately, you can only observe the physical pieces of the pattern, but the mental pieces are equally important. The rest of this book will detail what you should be doing at both levels of your 30-Second Swing—physical and mental.

Learning the 30-Second Swing is a major step in training your brain to play golf. Note that for purposes of clear explanation, the physical and mental are discussed separately, even though they are irrevocably joined in a seamless unit. One does not exist successfully without the other.

PATTERN OF THE 30-SECOND SWING

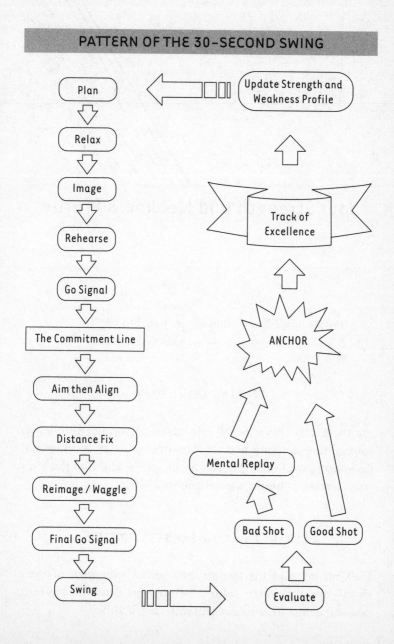

CHAPTER 2

Your Strength and Weakness Profile

People only see what they are prepared to see.
—Ralph Waldo Emerson

TAKING INVENTORY

Before you learn the 30-Second Swing you need to define your golfing strengths and weaknesses because an accurate and up-to-date profile can give you invaluable insight into the most vital element of hitting a good golf shot—*you.*

STRENGTH AND WEAKNESS PROFILE

I ask all my students to rate their ability with each of their clubs—driver through putter. Before you continue reading, take some time to rate your skill with each club.

Here are some typical answers given by students: "I hit my driver pretty well, my irons are okay, but I need work on my sand play." These are analog replies—general descriptions of your experience but not much help in developing a useful Strength and Weakness Profile. For example, if I ask you about the weather and you tell me that it's nice out, that's an analog reply. If you tell me it's 75 degrees Fahrenheit, the barometer is rising, and the wind is gusting at 12 miles per hour, that's a digital batch of information. Digital information is much more useful for certain types of decision-making, especially the decisions you need to make to play your best golf.

This is not to say that playing golf well involves only digital thinking. Golf is as much artistry as it is engineering but for the purposes of your Strength and Weakness Profile, I strongly advise you to gather as much digital information as you can from both your play and practice. Your brain loves digital information and its power to clarify muddled issues in your golf game, such as how good you really are with a particular club, is enhanced when you get specific.

In light of the above, it's obvious that you need to keep records so that your brain understands your strengths and weaknesses precisely. This way you'll be able to make your most accurate plans on the course, plans that produce Go signals because they favor your strengths. Keeping your stats also gives you a game plan for practice based on your play—you'll know what to practice by keeping track of your weaknesses as you play. You should split your practice time into two portions: devote just enough time to keeping your strengths current and the rest of the time to upgrading your weaknesses to strengths.

HOW DO YOU KNOW WHAT YOU DON'T KNOW?

In the December 1999 issue of the *Journal of Personality and Social Psychology*, Dr. David Dunning and Dr. Justin Kruger documented that most incompetent people do not know that they are incompetent, in part because the skills required for competence are the same skills necessary to recognize incompetence. This deficiency in "self-monitoring skills," Dunning says, "helps explain the tendency of the humor-impaired to persist in telling jokes that are not funny, of day traders to repeatedly jump into the market—and repeatedly lose out—and of the politically clueless to continue holding forth at dinner parties on the fine points of campaign strategy." And, we might add, the golfer who consistently overrates skills, such as his short game and how far he can hit the ball.

Other research indicates that overconfidence is quite common. For example, studies show that the majority of people rate themselves above average in a number of areas where they are not, begging the question, How do you know what you don't know, if you don't know it? The answer is, at least in golf, to digitize your experience—keep statistics!

TWO STRENGTH AND WEAKNESS PROFILES: PRACTICE AND PLAY

Golf courses are architects' prized possessions and they safeguard them by building in clever defenses. A major aspect of playing your best golf is fitting your Strength and Weakness Profile into the defenses set up by the architect. To do this you must make an accurate assessment of your playing skills, which are often different from your practice range skills. For this reason I encourage you to develop both a practice and a playing profile, and be sure you *never* confuse the two. Your playing profile reveals how well you perform when shot selection depends not only on the conditions but also on your ability to execute under the one-ball success rate, that is, a situation where every swing counts.

Tiger Woods can land a five-iron in a three-foot circle from 200 yards. Obviously his Strength and Weakness Profile is far different from that of most golfers. As you'll learn in the next chapter, though, no matter what your skill level is, to play your best consistently, you have to match your shot plan to your profile.

DEVELOPING A STRENGTH AND WEAKNESS PROFILE

Rate each of your clubs, using 3 for weak, 2 for average, and 1 for strong. If you like, add decimals like 1.5 to create a more sensitive range. In Chapter 4, you'll learn how to match these numbers to your plan. At first, your profile will be analog, but as you learn to use your PSO Scorecard, presented later in this chapter, your pool of statistics grows, and a more powerful digital profile emerges.

STRENGTH AND WEAKNESS PROFILE

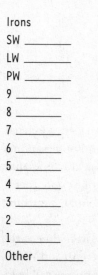

Irons
SW _____
LW _____
PW _____
9 _____
8 _____
7 _____
6 _____
5 _____
4 _____
3 _____
2 _____
1 _____
Other _____

Woods
Driver _____
3-wood _____
4-wood _____
5-wood _____
7-wood _____
Other _____

Other Shots
Short Putting _____
Lag Putting _____
Chipping _____
Chipping from Bermuda _____
Pitching _____
Pitching from Bermuda _____
Greenside bunker shots _____
Fairway bunker shots _____
From 100 yards _____ from 80 _____ from 60 _____
from 40 _____ from 20 _____
Uneven Lies
Ball above feet _____
Ball below feet _____
Uphill _____
Downhill _____

In addition to rating your clubs, it's helpful if you keep a journal where you record important golf experiences and observations, not only about your playing profile, but about anything that strikes your fancy. It is my belief that writing is not only therapeutic but also, since its form is linear and sequential, it encourages organized thinking.

To be the best player you can be at any given time, self-knowledge, in the form of a comprehensive Strength and Weakness Profile, is a necessity. The following questionnaire will help you increase your self-knowledge. Keep in mind that the better the player, the more accurately he or she can answer each of these questions. If you don't know the answers to a question, be sure that you take steps to find out.

CAN YOU WORK THE BALL?

Draw _____

Fade _____

High _____

Low _____

How good a wind player are you?

In general _____

Downwind _____

Headwind _____

Crosswind L to R _____

Crosswind R to L _____

What are your dragons (*mistakes and swing flaws that continually recur*)? _____

Describe your typical bad shot. _____

_____

Why do you think you hit this shot? _____

_____

What shot do you fear hitting the most? _____

Note: Because of their ability to compensate, better players often fear a shot other than their typical bad shot. For example, you may fear a hook but your typical miss is a block (straight right).

What is your miss pattern? _____

_____

Fat or thin _____

Hook or slice _____

Push or pull _____

Other _____

Medical Information

Any physical problems that affect your golf game? _____

_____

How's your vision? _____

Astigmatism? R _____ L _____

Contacts? _____

Bifocals when you play? _____

Which is your dominant eye? _____

Are you taking any medication that affects your stamina, balance, or vision? _____

Do you exercise? _____

Cardiovascular _____ Strength _____ Flexibility _____

Other sports? Current _____ Past _____

Are your clubs fit? _____ Off the rack? _____

Do you like them? Irons _____ Driver _____

Sand Wedge _____ Wedge _____ Fairway Woods _____

Putter _____ Other _____

Can you read your divots? _____

What do they say to you? _____

_____

Have you checked the lies of your clubs? _____ Recently? _____

Have you checked your lofts recently? _____

What is the composition of the ball you use? _____

What is its spin rate? _____

Why do you use this ball? _____

How far do you hit each of your clubs? _____

(Good players have three distance gradations for each club, as in a

little seven-iron, a regular seven, and a nuke seven. This allows a high-level player to cover all the distances encountered on the golf course. If your goal is to compete at the higher levels, you should practice this skill with all your clubs, including your driver.)

CASE HISTORIES THAT SHOW HOW TO USE THE STRENGTH AND WEAKNESS PROFILE

Bill Goes Balata

Bill is an 18 handicapper who uses a surlyn ball with a low spin rate because it flies farther and doesn't slice as much as a high-spin-rate balata ball. His former home course had large, soft greens but now he plays a course where the greens are firm and fast. Since joining the new course, his scores have risen. His Strength and Weakness Profile shows that his average number of greens hit in regulation is falling and he's not getting the ball up and down as often as he did at the old course.

There's a strong connection between these changing stats (missed greens and poor pitching). At the new course, many of his approach shots don't hold the slick greens, forcing him into more pitching situations than on the old course. Then his pitch shots jump out of the rough with very little spin, making it hard to stop the ball near the flag.

By analyzing his current Strength and Weakness Profile, he finds two significant ways to improve his game. First, he switches to a soft-cover balata ball that will hold the greens better and react more favorably on pitch shots, and his handicap returns to normal. Then he goes about fixing his slice, a weakness in his game that was masked, to some extent, by the surlyn ball.

Patty's Predicament

Patty is a high handicapper who, after keeping her stats, finds that all her long irons go about the same distance. In effect, she has three five-irons in her bag—the real five-iron, the four-iron, and the three-iron. She replaces the four- and three-iron with a seven- and nine-wood that are easier for a high handicapper to hit and her scores plummet.

Mismatched Mike

Mike is a single-digit handicapper whose stats reveal that he's missing a disproportionate number of greens to the left with his eight-iron. He has his lies checked and finds out that the reason he pulls his eight-iron is that it sits behind the ball with the toe too much in the air. He has it bent to match his other iron lies and the pull disappears.

Today we have machines that measure club specifications, but in the old days players picked clubs solely by feel and it often took them years to assemble a set with which they were comfortable. When Bobby Jones, the greatest player of his day, retired, he donated his clubs to a golf museum. Years later, just before he died, tests revealed that the only club in the set that was off was his eight-iron; the other irons were perfectly matched to one another. When Jones found out, he nodded and said, "I believe it, the eight was the only one of them I didn't like."

DEVELOP A CATALOG OF BEST SHOTS

Greg Norman has always referred to his Catalog of Best Shots: "You do want to file the good ones away for future reference. That way you'll be able to bring them back as part of another reinforcement technique—visualization. You envision the ideal shot, in detail. Then you recall successful similar shots from your past and draw confidence from those earlier successes. I can think of favorite shots for every situation I face and I call them forth each time I play."

In addition to digitizing your Strength and Weakness Profile, compile a catalog of the best shots you have ever hit, just as Norman does. Write down one for each club—the best driver, the best wedge; where, when, how did it feel? Further enhance your catalog by listing your best shots in challenging situations—in a tight match, against a heavy crosswind, over trees. . . . Then, in Chapter 3, when your plan calls for a high five-iron, you can mentally reference your Catalog of Best Shots and relive, for example, your best five-iron for an instant. Recall it with full imagery and then, with the feeling fresh in your imagination, let your body execute the shot free of any verbal conversation or instructions.

In Chapter 5, you'll learn how to prepare by fully imaging each shot from your catalog as part of your 30-Second Swing. Choose your representatives carefully. The most effective images are multisensorial—shots that make you recall the rhythm of the swing, the sound of contact, the sight of the ball in flight, or any other feature that makes the memory vivid. Whenever you play, be on the lookout for shots with sharper images that are better than those currently in your catalog. Replay your best shots in your mind until you burn them into your memory.

When your catalog is complete, and your recollection vivid, your brain will be stocked with the images necessary for you to play your best golf. All you have to do is step out of the way.

Best drive
Best putt
Best sand shot
Best trouble shot
Best long iron
Best middle iron
Best short iron

Best chip
Best pitch
And so on

GATHERING THE DATA—THE PSO SYSTEM

The PSO on-course tracking system is designed to keep your Strength and Weakness Profile current and your self-evaluation accurate and detailed. It will teach you to objectively evaluate each shot you hit based on your plan for the shot (P), your swing (S), and the outcome (O). Using this system you'll know which area of your game needs improvement: your planning or your swing.

The Plan

A good plan matches the desired outcome to your current capabilities in order to satisfy the conditions of the shot. Do you have your A, B, or C swing working that day? Is it a red-, green-, or yellow-light situation? What score do you need to make?

Once the shot is over, analyze your plan. Was it a good plan, a "smart play"? Could you go back to the spot and do it again? Or in retrospect was it a poor plan—even if it turned out okay? Sometimes you'll find that the opening for the punch shot through the trees was a lot smaller than it first appeared. At this stage of your PSO, the idea is to rate your planning ability, not your swing or the outcome.

If you hit the ball well on the course, but can't convert that to low scores, examine how well you plan. By evaluating your planning skills, you can discover any weakness you have behind the Commitment Line.

The Swing

Unfortunately, it's possible to receive a Go signal (see Chapter 5) and still make a bad swing. When you do, you'll know it. You'll say things like, "Boy, I thought I was going to hit it stiff, I don't know what went wrong," or, "I felt great over the ball and then it all fell apart." Since no golfer swings their best on every shot, your response to this situation is simply to record it as a bad swing. If it becomes a pattern (you hit the same weak shot more than twice), then list it as a weakness, and put it on your practice agenda.

You need to keep track of your bad swings (when, where, under what conditions) to check for patterns, but remember to do so without emotion. Just record the information, then deal with the bad swing by making another swing and anchor the correct feeling.

The Outcome

The shot that lands one foot from perfection, but comes to rest at the bottom of the lake, is categorized as a bad outcome. You have lost positional advantage, no matter how good the swing may have been. And that skulled shot that ran 120 yards along the ground before stopping three feet from the pin is a great outcome, no matter how bad the swing. You should have already mentally replayed the skulled shot so all you have to do is say something like, "Thank you, I accept the gift" (an auditory anchor) and make the putt. When less-than-perfect swings produce good outcomes (lucky breaks), many golfers are either too busy berating themselves or too embarrassed by their good fortune to take advantage of the situation. Don't be—anchor the good result as outlined in Chapter 9 and then make the putt!

PSO TRACKING SYSTEM

When you use the PSO, rate each element (plan, swing, and outcome) as follows:

0 = okay, not bad, great

1 = not good, bad, awful

To discover your potential for the game, use the following formula:

Score = Talent + PSO.

For example, you shot 80, with 10 bad outcomes, 25 bad plans, and 12 bad swings for a total PSO of 47.

80 = T + 47

or

T = (80 − 47) = 33

In this case, 33 is your Talent Index. The lower the PSO number, the closer you are to playing "perfect" golf for your current skill level. A perfect round would include no bad swings, no bad plans, and no bad outcomes, making your PSO = 0. But, given the nature of golf and the nature of human beings, perfection is rare. Also, keep in mind that plans, swings, and outcomes are relative. Tiger Woods's good outcome is a 315-yard drive down the middle. His bad outcome is a five-iron approach shot that lands 25 feet from the pin. That's different from a 20 handicapper whose good outcome is a 210-yard "fade" to the edge of the fairway, and bad outcome is a slice out of bounds. So just as your PSO is a function of your current skill, your Talent Index is a reflection of your current talent level. Both numbers are an indication of how well you are making use of your current skills.

When your Talent Index is low, it's time to take action to improve your game. If your Talent Index is high, it's time to pat yourself on the back and move to the next level, where you expect more from your PSOs.

The PSO system helps you keep your Strength and Weakness Profile current. In the above example, it's clear the player needs work on his shot planning.

PSO Scorecard

Use the PSO system and stat-keeping to digitize your Strength and Weakness Profile. When you have the time, rate your PSO for each shot you play on each hole. Enter zeros (0) for good plans, good swings, and good outcomes. Enter ones (1) for bad plans, bad swings, and bad outcomes. Add up your PSO rating and you'll quickly see your strengths and weaknesses.

In addition, enter your stats for each hole and add the totals after your round.

FIR = Fairway in Regulation (YES or NO)
GIR = Green in Regulation (YES or NO)
I # = Iron used for approach shot, or wood if that is the case
DFH = Distance from Hole—the distance your approach shot is from the hole
# P = Number of Putts
PR = Pin rating—Red (R), Yellow (Y), Green (G)

HOLE #1	1	2	3	4	5	6	7	TTL	STATS		Score = 6	
PLAN	0	1	0	1	1	0		3	FIR	NO	DFH	
SWING	1	0	0	0	0	0		1	GIR	NO	#P	3
OUTCOME	1	1	0	0	1	0		3	I#	SW	PR	R

HOLE #2	1	2	3	4	5	6	7	TTL	STATS		Score = 3	
PLAN	0	0	0						FIR	YES	DFH	
SWING	0	0	0						GIR	YES	#P	1
OUTCOME	0	0	0						I#	9	PR	G

HOLE #4	1	2	3	4	5	6	7	TTL	STATS		Score =	
PLAN									FIR		DFH	
SWING									GIR		#P	
OUTCOME									I#		PR	

HOLE #5	1	2	3	4	5	6	7	TTL	STATS		Score =	
PLAN									FIR		DFH	
SWING									GIR		#P	
OUTCOME									I#		PR	

CHAPTER 3

STAR

And remember, no matter where you go, there you are.

—CONFUCIUS

EVERYWHERE I GO, THERE I AM

TOMMY BOLT SAID that to be a player you have to own the club at the top of the swing, meaning that the club can't flop around out of control. The same is true for your golf behavior. To be a player, you must own your behavior on the golf course. If you don't, then you are simply performing on cue as the game of golf bombards you with stimuli such as wind, bad bounces, and a pressure-packed match.

If you can't run your brain, you'll play well when you receive favorable stimuli, but poorly when you encounter stimuli you've learned to interpret as unfavorable—and this is no way to play your best golf. This book is all about how to take control of your brain to improve the quality of your responses and therefore the quality of your outcomes.

This chapter will help you learn about your behavior as it relates to your golf game. Knowledge breeds control and, to be in control of your game, you have to take into consideration how you typically respond to the demands of the golf course, especially under pressure.

CHAMPIONS ARE IN CHARGE OF THEIR SUCCESS AND THEIR FAILURES

One caveat before we begin: Being in control of your response patterns does not guarantee that you will be successful every time. You plan for success, you prepare for it, and you expect it. You condition yourself to be successful and you're disappointed when you aren't even though you know there are times when you'll fail. The goal for every situation you face is to have such complete focus and such perfect preparation that all of your resources are brought to bear in a 100 percent effort. Then, if you fail, you know you have done your best and, in this way, your failure is under your control.

Look at it this way: A castaway adrift on a raft in the ocean has no control at all over which way he will go. He might wash ashore and survive, but it is none of his doing and he deserves no accolades. He could be swept out to sea and drown through no fault of his own, so he deserves no criticism. Either way, life or death, success or failure, he is a pawn, as out of control as any cork in the ocean.

But if you're a champion, you have a set of oars and a sail and, because you choose your responses, you are intimately and actively involved in the outcome. This is why I say that champions are in control not only of their successes but also their failures. Champions can and do fail, but it is not because they lost control of their responses; it is because the responses that they chose were not the ones necessary to win. As Napoleon said, "I have never been my own master. My master has always been the circumstances."

Champions evaluate the situation and create a response based on their Strength and Weakness Profile. Once they've decided their plan of action, the champion acts with total commitment, evaluates the outcome, and goes on to the next shot. Champions don't go against their own grain; they may be beat but they do not beat themselves.

WHO IS IN CONTROL?
In one way the golf course is a giant stimulus-response loop in which you can either be controlled by the stimuli or be in control of them. When you're in control, you organize, evaluate, and deal with the stimuli on your terms. If the wind is blowing 20 mph, instead of it ruining your game, you make it your friend, adapt your swing and your expectations. If you fail, you note wind play as a weakness and develop a plan to make it a strength.

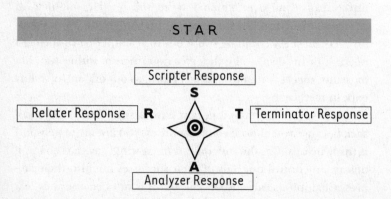

STAR

Scripter Response

S

Relater Response   R   T   Terminator Response

A

Analyzer Response

TURNING YOUR STAR

To help you understand your golf-related behavior, consider a construct fashioned after a four-point star, a behavioral compass that can serve as a guideline for golf self-analysis. STAR is an acronym for the four basic response patterns on your behavioral compass: Scripter, Terminator, Analyzer, and Relater. I created STAR not to describe the full complexities of human behavior, but as a tool that serves as a starting point for training your brain to adapt to changing golf situations—by changing the direction of your STAR.

> I believe we can change our everyday responses, and it's the sum of these incremental responses to everyday encounters that culminates in the abstraction called our personality or who we are. The question is, how will Y behave in X situation? The answer is, it depends. Those who talk like heroes could turn out to be cowards and those who seem like cowards could turn out to be heroes. A consistent response born of habit is one thing; a straitjacket called personality is another. I believe that habit and personality are often confused. Those who run their brains well escape this confusion.

In explaining STAR, I've tried to avoid using the term *personality* since STAR is not an index to measure personality. Many experts believe that except for minor changes, the adult personality is fixed and they promote testing instruments to support their theories. The question is, what do these instruments really measure? If you assume there is an entity called personality and define how to measure personality, then the measurement device (such as a questionnaire) contains a built-in bias since the definition you started with controls the content of the questionnaire. Change your definition of personality, change the questions, or ask them in a different way, and you get different results.

A student of mine took a personality test that was one of the most validated instruments of its kind. He retook the test five years later and was impressed that the results were the same. He took this to mean that his personality hadn't changed; I took it to mean that he answered the same questions in the same way. He took it to mean that he had a specific personality type; I took it to mean that whatever the questions were designed to measure, they measured "it" and "it" hadn't changed.

In my opinion, the more you analyze the concept of personality the more amorphous it becomes until it finally dissolves. Besides which it is a wonder to me how so much faith can be placed in the written or spoken word. The theory seems to be that if you want to know what a person is all about, ask them. This assumes that there is a direct line from the tongue to the truth and we know from our own simple experience that this isn't the case.

RESPONSE PATTERNS

Each point on the STAR represents a typical response pattern to whatever stimulus is present. Like a compass that responds to magnetic pull, you can control your responses by learning to rotate your STAR based on the situations you encounter on the golf course. As the situation changes, your STAR turns to the appropriate response pattern.

The champion chooses the best response by controlling which point on the STAR they will use to face the situation. Champions can actually turn their STAR by the sheer power of their will. The nonchampion (regardless of talent level) doesn't control where the STAR faces and in most cases the STAR either spins out of control under a barrage of stimuli, or is frozen in place until it is too late. Being able to control your STAR is a huge part of being able to train your brain. Once your swing has enough technical excellence to be reliable, control of your STAR system becomes an essential resource.

HABIT AND COMPULSION

Whatever else the human being is, it is a stimulus-response animal. When the stimulus is quickly followed by the response, with no space in between, it's called a habit or, in its more advanced stage, a compulsion. There is no time for reflection and, therefore, no choice is possible. Your STAR is stuck and every time a particular stimulus occurs, you can expect the same response.

In golf, the flagstick represents a stimulus since the flagstick signifies the hole location, your final destination. If your only response to the flagstick is to attack—regardless of its position, your skill level, or the conditions of play—then there is no space between the stimulus and the response, and the stimulus is running your brain.

But it's possible to have a space separating the stimulus and the response. This space provides a reflective period necessary to make a choice. It gives you, as outlined below, time to turn your STAR, an essential maneuver that every champion has to learn.

STAR POINTS

[S] Scripter—Idealist, above-it-all, committed
[T] Terminator—Aggressive, leader, action-oriented
[A] Analyzer—Methodical, calculating, efficient
[R] Relater—Social, optimistic, unflappable

When you turn your STAR to face a certain situation, you are then in that response pattern. So if your STAR point is on Scripter, then you are in Scripter mode; if it's on Terminator, then you are in Terminator mode, etc.

Though you're a combination of all four modes, many golfers form habits that can take their responses to the extreme. For example, the Terminator can become too aggressive under the stress of highly competitive golf, turning a major strength into a downfall. As we've already seen, Greg Norman periodically self-destructs under pressure, not because he chokes, but because he becomes far too aggressive. By attempting shots too risky for the circumstances, Norman has often snatched heartbreaking defeat from the jaws of victory. His downfall occurs when he lets his strength (fearlessness) evolve into a weakness (foolhardiness).

FLEXIBILITY EQUALS SURVIVAL

If you recognize your STAR options, you'll know when to rotate your compass to the response pattern best suited to control the circumstances. You switch clubs as the situation changes, so why not switch response patterns? Just as a chameleon eludes predators by changing color to blend with its background, you can adapt your behavior to suit the conditions and circumstances of play. Your behavior dictates how you play the game every bit as much as the quality of your swing, your physical condition, and your equipment. Adaptation is the chameleon's key to survival and it is a golfer's key to success.

With maturity comes the versatility to deal effectively with a wide range of situations. Sometimes in the brashness of youth, where bravado and daring substitute for flexibility and good judgment, the STAR stays too long on one point. Many Senior PGA Tour players echo Jim Thorpe's comments after he shot 69 and 65 in the first two rounds of the 2000 U.S. Senior Open. "I'm a much better ball striker now," Thorpe said. "Back then, I was young and strong and I tried to hit the ball a mile. Now, even though I can hit a seven-iron from 180 yards, I know enough about the game to know I don't have to."

EACH PERSON IS A STAR

The STAR message is one of freedom. Each person is a STAR and has all four points available to them. Learning to turn your STAR is an important part of running your brain because it gives you the flexibility to handle any situation—it's your can-do system. Acting as though you have a fixed "personality" is the antithesis of running your own brain because it confines you to certain preordained responses—a "can't-do" system. This is why good brain runners keep their STAR liquid while poor ones let it freeze up.

The problem is that under stress, the STAR can lock up and be unable to swivel. When your STAR freezes on one setting too long, you can't adapt to the changing situation. The first step in keeping your STAR fluid is the knowledge that, to be a good player, you must.

MAXIMIZE YOUR RETURN

Following is a description of each point on your STAR. When you are running your brain well, you choose the STAR response that maximizes your control over the situation. This does not mean that you win every time or that you always dominate; it means that given the circumstances, conditions, and the state of your game, you get the most out of each situation. As soon as the situation changes, your STAR swivels to a new point on the compass to bring to bear a new way of responding that allows you to enhance your yield from the interaction. Anyone can do this—all it takes is practice.

A LIFE SCORE

The ultimate barometer of how well your STAR system is functioning is the record of your outcomes. There's a story, supposedly true, of a man who kept a daily record of his experiences and rated the outcomes for each with a plus (+) or a minus (−). A modest success might receive a ++, a great outcome a +++++++++, a very bad outcome a −−−−−−−−−−−−− and so on. As he lay dying, he asked his son to total up his life score. After going through a trunkful of his father's notebooks, he returned to his father's deathbed with the tally. "On the whole," he whispered to his father, "it was a slight plus."

MULTIPLE PERSONALITIES?

For the champion, though, a slight plus total is not good enough. As a champion brain runner, who you are depends on what situation you're in. Sometimes you're an idealist with the broad sweep—it's life, liberty and the pursuit of happiness; other times you think in columns and the numbers have to add up. In one situation you're mad as hell and aren't going to take it anymore, while in another it's live and let live. This is not being wishy-washy; it's being flexible and, in this regard, we all have (or should have) the multiple personalities described below in the STAR construct.

YOUR SCRIPTER POINT

S stands for the Scripter mode, the classic idealist response with a life script that must be followed. Karl Marx, Martin Luther, and Joan of Arc spent a lot of time in the S mode. When S takes the point, experiences are filtered through a code or blueprint of how the world should be that shows where everything and everybody fits in. In your Scripter response mode, you are on a quest to right wrongs. You become indignant with something as local as an able-bodied person parking in handicap parking, or as global as oppression of the worker or an unfair tax on tea.

When you're in S, you divide the population into black hats and white hats, and people are either part of the problem or part of the solution. Your search for perfection makes it hard for you to make commitments. "If I commit to this," you think, "and there is something better, more righteous, or more perfect, I will have taken the wrong course and violated my high standards." However, in Scripter mode, once you commit to a code or a quest, you are a dogged opponent, a powerful proselytizer, and a faithful friend.

Having found a worthy code, you're bold and assertive, sometimes bordering on domineering. While not pleasant, this behavior makes sense since you subscribe to a code you believe everyone should follow. With this code in hand, you make it your job to get the word out.

In S, you fear boredom and having to follow a leader who moves too methodically. Therefore, although you don't want the headaches of being the boss, you do want to exert the influence of the leader. You're behind the scenes and out of the limelight but you want to run the show.

Fictional characters whose one-dimensional behavior is created to fit a role in a story often have prototypical responses that match the points on the STAR. For the Scripter point, we have characters such as Robin Hood, Don Quixote, Sir Lancelot, Hercules, the Lone Ranger, Batman, and Indiana Jones.

Your S Golf Profile

When you are in S, you're cordial on the course, but not overly social unless you're in the company of a close friend—then you relax and open up. You don't often stay around for the postgolf beer-and-sympathy routine; you're much more likely to retreat to the privacy of your home.

In your S mode, you're serious about your golf game. Golf is not just a game for you, it's a testing ground where success and failure become barometers of your self-esteem. You're loyal to the game itself, its history, its tradition, and especially its rules. You despise cheaters, blowhards, and sandbaggers, not to mention golfers who wear their hats backward and spectators who shout, "You da man!"

Your S Strengths

When you're in your S mode and things are going as they should on the course, you play your best. With your swing grooved, you're proud of the hard work you've done to bring your game to this level. The improvement process is a long-term affair, and you stuck it out. You feel it's only fair that all your hard work should yield a good return, and you are upset when it doesn't pan out that way.

Only when you feel your swing mechanics are sound do you expect to play your best golf. In S mode, you like to practice—work toward the ideal—almost more than you like to play. Your sessions are long and frequent, and you're always on the lookout for ways to improve your swing.

Your S Weaknesses:
It's Time to Turn Your STAR When . . .

When you overdo your S, it's time to turn your STAR. One warning sign is the tendency to spend most of your golf career "getting ready" on the practice range and very little of your time actually playing.

Another sign is an overheightened sense of fairness; when this happens, you have great difficulty accepting both your bad luck and your opponent's good luck, either of which can ruin your game. To play your best golf you need to accept the fact that luck (both bad and good) is a part of the game. You may not be able to control luck, but you can control your response to it by turning the STAR so that your Analyzer points straight at the problem. The Analyzer perceives luck as a statistical event with no cosmic message attached to it. Instead of treating luck as something external that forces its way in and violates the script, luck is an integral part of the script. Use of your Analyzer mode here will maximize your return. As Jack Nicklaus said when asked about a particularly bad break: "Nobody ever said this game was fair."

Another clue that your S is out of control is when you become upset when you lose to someone with a sorry-looking swing—an injustice that violates a Scripter's sense of fairness. Your concept in S is, may the best swing win, a concept that can cause you endless grief. You need to white out the part of your script that reads, "The hardest worker with the best swing should always win." Condition yourself that as soon as you see one of those funky homemade swings, your response is to rotate to your Terminator point on the STAR and get tough. You need to embrace the "it's not how, but how many" philosophy; forget about both his swing and yours and just go kick butt.

In 1938, Paul Runyan won his second PGA Championship by defeating Sam Snead. The fact that Runyan won is not amazing—he was a great player—but the manner in which he won was amazing. Runyan crushed Snead 8 and 7 in the championship match (he was eight holes ahead with only seven left to play), one of golf's classic David versus Goliath tales. Runyan was by no means a long hitter, but Snead was about the longest of his era. Runyan was a short-game wizard and his style of play drove Snead crazy.

Another indication that it's time to turn your STAR is when you buy into the concept that since you've worked hard and put in your time, you deserve to play well. Don't fall into that logic. Turn your STAR to Analyzer for the antidote: "Only people owe people—golf is a game, and it owes you nothing."

The belief that your game is gone for good is also a prime-time indicator that your compass needs to turn away from S. At a low point in his young career Lee Westwood, who became one of the top-ranked players in the world, had lost all hope. This is typical of a STAR stuck in S and an indication that their script needs a bit of a rewrite. "I'm losing interest very quickly . . ." a deflated Westwood said. "I just can't see where the next good round is coming from . . . I don't know what to do. I don't really feel like playing because I can't compete."

Two weeks later he won the European Tour's biggest prize: (E450,000) in the Deutsche Bank Open. That victory also made him only the second golfer to catch Tiger Woods after Woods held the fifty-four-hole lead. How did Westwood work this miracle turnaround—from the outhouse to the penthouse? He turned his STAR to its Relater point by acting on some advice from his teacher David Leadbetter. "David didn't give me too much to think about in the way of technique," Westwood explained. "I think he could tell that most of my problems were inside my head. He told me just to go out and enjoy myself . . . I know now that no matter how deep a slump I'm in, there is no need to panic."

The game of golf is riddled with script wreckers. Just when you have it figured, and you've written it down nice and neat, preserved for all time, it vanishes. And when you're sure your game has gone for good, it suddenly reappears. This kind of whimsy is unsettling and the danger is that you will come to view the golf course as an unsafe place where something bad can happen—for no reason at all.

YOUR TERMINATOR POINT

T stands for Terminator, the aggressive, take-charge, dominating point on your STAR. World War II General George S. Patton, whose STAR spent much of its time on T, responded to a warning about the strong Nazi defenses in Europe by saying, "We're going to run through the Germans like shit through a goose."

Others who spend a good deal of time in T are basketball behemoth Shaquille O'Neal, who has Superman's S tattooed on his arm; legendary daredevil Evel Knievel, who broke just about every bone in his body during his career; and Amelia Earhart, who lost her life in pursuit of daring achievement.

When you're in T, you're easily annoyed and you often resort to confrontation to solve a problem. You're impatient and independent and it's your way or the highway. While you may be hard to get along with unless others go along, you are good to have around when the going gets tough.

Fictional characters that depict the Terminator are Captain Ahab, Captain Kirk, Dirty Harry, Rambo, Moby Dick, and, of course, the Terminator himself.

Your T Golfing Profile

In T, you're a fearless gambler who announces on the 1st tee, "I'll play you for five dollars, and you two for ten." You're a full-speed-ahead, grip-it-and-rip-it type who smashes your driver and hunts the flag. You play with anyone who can give you a game, or give you an opportunity to go on display. You relish the starring role. Players like Ray Floyd, Tiger Woods, Greg Norman, and John Daly all spend a lot of time in T.

When you're in T, you're an assertive, action-oriented golfer who can become impatient if your game doesn't progress fast enough. Slow play drives you crazy. You become bored easily and have a short attention span. When pushed, you push back and worry about the consequences later. When the consequences arrive, you greet them with even more aggressive tactics.

When your STAR point is on T, you'd rather play than practice, and prefer match to medal play. You're not much for taking lessons, though you freely give advice—solicited or not. When you do take a lesson, it had better be long on the doing and short on the explaining. Forget the drills and teaching aids; you're there to hit golf balls, and hit 'em better. Your time frame for improvement: now, if not sooner.

Greg Norman was in T when a jeweler in Palm Beach Gardens, Florida, was charged with defrauding customers of more than $80 million, Jack Nicklaus ($380,000) and Norman ($350,000) among them. When Nicklaus discovered the problem, he had his lawyers file suit—an Analyzer response. When Norman found out, he went directly to the dealer's showroom, confronted him, and got his money back.

Your T Strengths

You're a fearless flag hunter who can hit great shots and shoot low numbers for your handicap when you're on a roll in your T mode. You use momentum to bring a golf course or an opponent to its knees. You're tough, especially in a scramble format where you can lead the team and be the hero. You can be a terror in a skins game or match play because you never give up. You exude confidence. Your battle cry is, "The pins can hide but they can't run." When you're on your game you play big, talk big, and bet big—always pushing the envelope. For you, it's not how but how many. You don't care much about how your swing looks; how it works is what's important.

Your T Weaknesses:
It's Time to Turn Your STAR When . . .

When your T is out of control and ego rules the day, you can't acknowledge your weaknesses, which is itself a serious weakness. As demonstrated earlier, to play your best golf you must have an accurate Strength and Weakness Profile. But when you hit driver where two-iron is the choice, and when you shoot at sucker flags when you should play safely to the center of the green, your overaggressiveness inevitably leads to a bogey, or worse. With your momentum broken, you get angry and even more aggressive—a bad combination that leads to more hawkish mistakes.

Impatience is a sign your STAR needs turning. When T is on the point, patience is not your virtue. You play fast, and get mad when the pace of play slows. In an effort to learn patience, one PGA Tour player, wise enough to realize that his STAR was stuck on T, drove around Palm Springs, California, purposely staying behind elderly drivers moving at a snail's pace. If impulsiveness is ruining your game, you need to do whatever it takes to add the strength of patience to your response patterns on the golf course.

No one ever swiveled his STAR better than Tiger Woods during the 2000 U.S. Open. Paul Azinger said, "I think some people said he didn't have the game to win a U.S. Open. . . . But whenever you put the onus on a guy like that, he shows up." And show up he did, first in T with an aggressive 65, which then allowed him to switch to his A mode at the least provocation. After his workmanlike third-round 71, featuring a triple bogey on the 3rd hole that could have sent a lesser STAR spinning out of control, Woods revealed his strategy. "If I went out there and was patient and hit a lot of fairways and greens I knew I'd make a putt here and there and maybe increase my lead and let them know it was almost impossible to catch me."

In excess T, you avoid lessons when your swing falls apart and try to fix the problem by yourself. This can lead to disaster and put you out of commission for longer than the normal swing breakdown should. When this happens, turn to your Analyzer mode to allow for more systematic thinking. Find an instructor who can put you back on track with minimal theory and swing mechanics. Tell him you like your swing but need it tweaked.

And while you're turning your STAR, don't forget to stop at Relater and enjoy the social aspect of the game. After you've hit your shot, and in between beating the course into submission, "Stop and smell the roses," as Walter Hagen advised.

YOUR ANALYZER POINT

A stands for Analyzer, a response pattern where you're organized and systematic. People who spend a lot of time in A are the accountants, engineers, and programmers of the world, people with outward manifestations of orderliness such as Alan Greenspan, Albert Einstein, Madame Curie, and Jack Nicklaus. They think in columns, and make decisions based on how the numbers add up. When you're in A, you save your receipts, play by the rules, and go by the book, from which you can recite chapter and verse.

In A, your goal is to come up with the right answer using sound logic. Standard Operating Procedure is your bible. You appear contemplative and cerebral in this mode and you wield an objective fact like a sword to cut through confusion and stupidity. Intellect is your name and numbers are your game.

Fictional characters that define the A mode are Silas Marner, Perry Mason, Sherlock Holmes, Mr. Spock, Ebenezer Scrooge, Dick Tracy.

Your A Golf Profile

In A, you're a deliberate planner in complete control of your emotions. Golf greats Ben Hogan and Jack Nicklaus used the A mode perfectly: meticulous in their preparations, patient in competition, unflappable in the face of danger or surprise, and master strategists. When your A is working well you know your golf game in detail and play golf with attention to its every facet, including practice, skill refinement, and careful preparation.

Here is an example of a champion functioning in A. The week before his historic performance in the 2000 U.S. Open at

Pebble Beach, Tiger Woods spent three full days on the practice range with his swing coach, Butch Harmon. "We didn't have anything to fix in Tiger's swing," Harmon explained, "we just had to shape some shots, curve the ball a bit differently for some of the holes out there."

And once he arrived at Pebble Beach, Tiger was in Analyzer mode when he needed to be. "I didn't like the way the ball was rolling into the hole. . . . The ball wasn't turning over the way I like to see the ball rolling." So after his first round he went to the practice green for two hours to get it right—a round in which he shot 65 and had twenty-four putts!

Your A Strengths

With your STAR turned to A, you're an excellent course manager, and have a disciplined approach to your practice and play. You get mad, just like the next guy, but seldom lose your cool for more than a few seconds. Reason guides you at all times and keeps you from making stupid mistakes or angry blunders.

You're in control of your emotions and your game because you make a plan and stick to it. You'll hit an iron off the tee to stay in play when your swing is off, and you don't mind laying up short of trouble instead of attempting a risky carry. You're analytical, but if something goes wrong with you swing while you're playing you don't panic and tinker yourself to death. Jack Nicklaus said, "I never conduct full-scale swing analysis or try to make big changes on the course itself. It's better to make the best of whatever you have at the moment than risk compounding problems by attempting major surgery."

In A, you're an excellent student and learn very quickly as long as the teacher is logical and answers your questions satisfactorily. You like organized and structured presentations and the concept you're learning must add up before you commit to the change.

Your A Weaknesses:
It's Time to Turn Your STAR When . . .

It's time to turn your STAR when you begin to suffer from lack of intuition and imagination. When you're stuck in A, you play it a little too close to the vest, sticking to your game plan even after it becomes obvious that it's not working. A classic example was Chip Beck's decision to lay up during the last round of the 1993 Masters. The 15th is a short par-5 and Beck had about 200 yards to the front of the green and 235 yards to the pin. He was trailing leader Bernhard Langer and needed to get back in the hunt. Langer, in the group behind him, still had the 15th to play. With a good lie and the firepower to reach the green in two and putt for eagle, he elected instead to follow his game plan and lay up, a decision that all but handed the Masters to Langer.

Remember it's a plan, not the only plan, and it's only as good as the situation it was designed for. When that situation changes, the plan must change. If your opponent is making an unprecedented number of birdies and you're sticking with "fairway-green-two-putts-par," you're going to be trampled.

Lessons in A

As a student with an analytical mind, you can easily go overboard with the questions when you're taking a lesson. Balance your A with some grip-it-and-rip-it T or a social dose from your R mode. The worst problem in A is thinking too much about swing mechanics while you play. If you do, you'll have trouble taking "it" to the course. To avoid paralysis by analysis on the golf course, you have to forget mechanics and focus on the target. In this case, a little T-style target hunting can be just the ticket.

YOUR RELATER POINT

R stands for Relater, the public persona epitomized by Arnold Palmer, Robin Williams, Will Rogers, Maria von Trapp, and Ronald Reagan. When you're in R you're a social animal, a feel-good, have-fun, sooner-rather-than-later person. Problem solving is tomorrow's chore. In this mode, you can chat with anyone and you make everyone feel good. You tell people what they want to hear, not to be devious, but because you want everyone to enjoy their time with you as much as you enjoy your time with them.

In R, you can be capricious, changing your mind and switching your priorities. You can be tough, but your hard bargain is delivered with a sweet smile and the velvet touch. And you're approachable even if you're famous. Just about everyone who has had the privilege of being in an Arnold Palmer gallery felt Arnold's magical charm making them feel like they were the King's old friend.

When you're in R, you're understanding and appear to truly like and trust people. When your STAR points to R, you attract many friends who tell you their troubles because you're a good listener and tolerant of their failings.

Fictional characters that epitomize the R mode are Santa Claus, Dr. Doolittle, Rob Petrie, Andy of Mayberry, the Good Witch, Bugs Bunny, Winnie-the-Pooh, Dorothy, Roger Rabbit, Mr. Chips, and June and Ward Cleaver.

Your R Golf Profile

With your STAR on R you're outgoing and enthusiastic—a talker, a joiner, a socializer. Friday afternoon at work you say, "I'll play if you do, Joe! And call Bill and Jenny to see if they can join us." In R, golf is playtime for you. You're the first to console playing partners disgusted with their performance, and always remind them that it's only a game. You're also the first to praise a great shot, even if it puts you at a competitive disadvantage.

In Relater mode, Walter Hagen's reminder to "stop and smell the roses" gives you pause. "Why stop?" you say. "I enjoy the roses all the time." Part of the joy of golf is the beauty of your surroundings, which is second only to the camaraderie inherent to the game.

In your R mode, you're lesson taker because you're open to new ideas, other people's opinions, and, of course, the friendly interaction with the instructor. That's the good news. On the other hand, practicing what you've learned is boring and lonely, so your swing fixes can disappear in a hurry, and so can your game. You'll excel most rapidly with a teacher who makes the lessons fun without a lot of drills and drudgery. Your goal is to play the game better, not to perfect your swing. On the professional level those who spend a lot of time in R are Arnold Palmer, Peter Jacobsen, Chi Chi Rodriguez, Gary McCord, and David Feherty.

Your R Strengths

Almost everyone enjoys your company on the course when you're in your Relater mode, and you're never at a loss to find a game. Under pleasant circumstances, you play your best. You're flexible and adaptable so disruptions don't rattle your game. But bad weather and cutthroat games leave you cold. You're not afraid of tough competition, but in your R you treat golf as a game, not a battle. In your ideal round, everyone plays well and enjoys themselves. If your match is all square after 18, your inclination is to forget the playoff and go have a drink. You certainly don't like to lose, but neither is it fun for you to win if you make an enemy or upset someone.

You play at the pace established by your foursome or the course, and you adjust easily when the going gets slow. You'd prefer not to play with a Terminator or the resident grouch, but you can play your game with anyone. You have other things to fall back on . . . like those roses. When you're in R, golf is a game to take pleasure from, not a barometer of your self-esteem.

Your R Weaknesses:
It's Time to Turn Your STAR When . . .

You have to be careful in R because course management can become a weakness—you're too busy chatting and enjoying the scenery to pay strict attention to your game. Unfortunately, if you're not having fun, you can lose interest completely and your game collapses. To prevent this from happening, turn your STAR to A and make sure you go through your entire routine for every shot. This way you'll have to focus for about 30 seconds per shot and the rest of the time you can socialize.

It's definitely time to rotate points when you lose a match because you lack that killer instinct. When you're one up, you're content because you're winning, but not hurting anyone too badly. Unfortunately, this can leave the door open for your opponent to come from behind and bite you. You need to call on the Terminator, whose response to being one up is to try to go two up.

And you know it's time to turn your STAR when you take tips from any source, professional or amateur, even if the amateur source has a handicap 15 strokes higher than yours. This behavior is one of the best ways to ruin your swing, so when it comes to lessons, point your STAR to Scripter and become more long term oriented. Find a teacher you like and develop a blueprint to give you a solid platform on which to build your game.

A STAR ENCOUNTER WITH TIGER WOODS

Imagine four people at the 19th hole, each in a different STAR setting. In walks golf idol Tiger Woods. The person in Terminator rushes up and insists on buying Tiger a drink, while loudly offering his opinion of Tiger's competitive record. He's certain Tiger's spirits will be boosted by his glowing appraisal. To show his knowledge, he asks Tiger about a situation in the 1998 Masters on the 17th hole. As Tiger begins to answer, he interrupts him to give Tiger his own rendition of the event. . . .

The person in Relater gives Tiger a friendly pat on the arm and asks for his autograph. He tells a funny story while Tiger signs his name. The R smiles and nods in approval at Tiger's every word. They trade do-you-know-so-and-so's and have a wonderful chat. . . .

The Analyzer remains in her seat to develop a plan for meeting the superstar by studying both the T's and the R's encounters with Tiger. When the time is right, she walks briskly to Tiger, offers her rehearsed greeting, makes a succinct statement of admiration, and returns to her seat to await further developments.

The Scripter watches it all, and shakes her head at the T's boldness. The S waits in the background, never acknowledging the presence of the best golfer on the planet with a look in his direction. As Tiger is leaving, the S times it perfectly so she crosses in front of Tiger, nods, and Woods returns the nod. That's all, and it is enough for a person in the Scripter mode.

CHAPTER 4

The Plan

Piglet kept worrying and worrying about being lost in the forest. Pooh said nothing. Finally Rabbit decided to forage off on his own, and when he left, Pooh said, "Now, then, Piglet, let's go home." "But Pooh," cried Piglet all excited, "do you know the way?" "No," said Pooh, "but there are 12 honey pots in my cupboard and they've been calling to me for hours. I couldn't hear them properly before because Rabbit would talk, but if nobody says anything except those 12 honey pots, I think, Piglet, I shall know where they're calling from."

—BENJAMIN HOFF, *The Tao of Pooh*

TO EXCEL AT GOLF, you must have an accurate Strength and Weakness Profile, and then fit that profile into the defenses set up by the architect, given the circumstances and conditions of play. This chapter is about developing a plan, a mental map that tells you where you are going and how you will get there.

Tomasi demonstrating the plan

THE PLANNING POSITION

Your 30-Second Swing begins three to four strides behind the
ball where you're looking down the target line and focusing on
where you want the ball to go. From this position, you'll begin
to formulate your shot plan. This position is universal among
great players and, because of the arrangement of our eyes, it is a
position every golfer should emulate.

Eyes on the Side of Your Head?

For a million years, the brain has made a living tracking important targets like lions and tigers and bears, so rest assured, you have an expert on board. But to locate targets, your brain needs accurate information and in golf that requires positioning your visual system where it functions the best—looking directly down the target line.

If your body had been specifically designed for golf, you'd have both eyes on the target side of your head so that when you assumed your stance to the side of the ball, you could see the target straight on. Since we don't, every good player makes his or her plan behind the ball to take advantage of the most accurate form of visual data collection—straight-ahead binocular vision.

At the back of the eye on the retina are groups of "seeing cells." These cells are most densely packed in an area called the fovea, making it the area of greatest visual acuity, ideal for tracking important things like targets. Foveal vision has the advantage of depth perception, a feature that is highly useful when it comes to hunting flagsticks and fairways. So it is for a good reason that experts stand behind the ball to make their plan where they can secure a "foveal fix" on the target.

As you move away from the fovea, the seeing cells thin out and it becomes progressively more difficult to locate and identify objects precisely. This is your peripheral vision and its primary purpose is to identify motion. Golfers who try to locate the target standing to the side of the ball are likely to have a distorted view and therefore to mislocate it. For this reason, you position yourself behind the ball in the planning stage of your 30-Second Swing.

MAKING YOUR PLAN

Ben Hogan called golf a game of adjustments, and he wasn't just referring to tweaking his golf swing or taking a bit off a six-iron. Hogan recognized that golf requires constant reevaluation of conditions like the wind and the lie of the ball, and the effect they have on a golf shot. These adjustments require the total concentration necessary for locating the target, evaluating its defenses (bunkers, water, trees, etc.) and then developing a strategy for getting from point A to point B based on your current resources. This process is necessary for each shot you hit, and that can be mentally tiring. If you lose your focus on a few shots during a round, your score inches up. If you fail to plan most of your shots correctly, the wheels fall off.

One of the reasons golf is so fascinating is that the adjustments are endless. Like snowflakes, no two shots are ever the same because you change and so does the playing field. Your blood sugar level changes, your electrolyte balance fluctuates, your cell phone delivers a heart-stopping margin call, and an unlucky bounce out of bounds makes your blood pressure soar. Every lie is different; every angle to the pin is new. For one shot the wind is behind you; on the next, it's blowing left; and on another, it dies completely as the ball takes flight.

One factor remains consistent, however. You have to make specific, well-planned adjustments for every shot you face. Case in point: The legendary par-3 12th at Augusta is only an eight-iron away for the average PGA Tour player, but no amount of eight-irons struck perfectly in practice can prepare a player for the swirling winds at Amen Corner. You have to make the adjustments on the spot.

It's ironic that you practice the normal on the driving range but face the abnormal on the golf course. On the driving range, there is no water and there are no sidehill lies or trees. If you're like most golfers, you pick a spot with the best grass and the most level ground and then hit thirty-five six-irons in a row. A half hour later you're on the course, ready to hit your first six-iron of the round, but now the ball is below your feet, the lie is thin, and the wind gusting. Physically it may look like the same club, but this six-iron is far different from the six-irons you hit on the range and, if you can't make the adjustments, you can't make the play.

Eyes in Front

There is a theory that the eyes of predators are located at the front of the head so they can spot prey, while the eyes of prey are to the side of the head to better track the predators. By this definition, then, human beings are predators—target hunters who need accurate information about the world. To gather that information you locate the target on your mental grid—its latitude, longitude, and depth. You reach out and embrace the target with your senses, serving as a receiving station for information flowing from the target about its location and its defenses. You site the target in the crosshairs with your tracking channels wide open—just like a baseball fielder catching a fly ball.

Why an Outfielder Wears Sunglasses

At the crack of the bat the center fielder is off and running. He looks up into the sun and flips down his sunglasses to locate the ball against a brilliant blue sky. After running 30 yards he waits at the warning track, pats his glove a couple of times, and makes the catch. A simple, routine play, but what actually transpired in the fielder's brain was far from simple.

An article in *The New York Times* described a mathematician's effort to calculate the odds of a center fielder catching a fly ball. The scientist broke the event down into all its component parts—the distance of the fielder from home plate, the arc of the ball's flight, the brain's calculations of the intercept point, the muscles involved in running, raising the arm, opening the fingers, and closing the hand around a ball that is plummeting to earth at 32 feet per second squared. His conclusion: Statistically, it couldn't be done! And it can't, unless the outfielder's visual tracking system is working—that's why he wears sunglasses—to keep the channels that track his prey open and receptive.

TRACKING SYSTEMS

Of our five senses, golf's "big three" are visual, kinesthetic, and auditory, and the visual system reigns supreme. Approximately 30 percent of the fibers from the optic nerve connect to brain regions other than those devoted to vision. These regions include your balance system, your motor cortex, and your emotional centers. Like vision, each of these plays a role in hitting a ball to a target. The visual system, however, dominates the act of locating objects in time and space, determining not only where and what it is but if the object is moving toward you or away.

The kinesthetic system is a secondary tracking system that enables you to locate and identify an object based on characteristics such as its shape and texture. However, this system is more than simply tactile. It also provides a feel, or sense, for what's going on inside your body. When you move a muscle, stretch a tendon, or rotate a joint, your brain monitors the action and tracks the motion.

Another feature of the kinesthetic system is that it produces feelings far subtler than physical touch. When you look at somebody you care about, the image prompts certain feelings, perhaps the feeling that your heart is about to jump out of your chest. As a golfer when you stand on the 17th tee at TPC Sawgrass, that same heart may skip a beat. As you'll see in the last chapter, these feelings are evoked not only by the present stimulus, they are also a product of past experiences.

The third of the big three is the auditory tracking system. This ingenious component for personal survival allows you to locate the source of a sound, and identify how close it is and whether it's moving toward or away from you.

These tracking systems, as well as the others you have on board, are all coordinated into a weblike matrix so finely integrated that each system influences the others. Information that floods in from one source is shared with your other tracking systems so that matters of utmost importance, such as the survival of the species and the well-being of your golf game, can flourish.

DON'T FOOL WITH THE FOOLPROOF PROCESS

For years, it was a puzzle. How did sea turtles navigate huge expanses of ocean and arrive at their destination with such uncanny accuracy? Scientists discovered a program in the turtles' brains that calculates longitude and latitude based on the angle and intensity of the magnetic field on the ocean floor. With this tiny neural chip, the turtle finds its annual target—a sea turtle convention 2,000 miles away. So if the turtle can find its target halfway around the globe, why can't you hit your ball into a $4\frac{1}{4}$-inch hole from 10 feet—what's going on here? Well, the turtle doesn't try to think its way to the convention; it goes there automatically. And there are a lot of things that you can do much better if you'd just put the system on automatic and stop getting involved.

That's why you can walk across a footwide board resting on the ground without a problem, but when it's suspended 200 feet in the air, it's a different story. In the first instance, you let your unconscious competence handle the act of walking and it's a piece of cake; in the second, the "fool" is back on the job and you're in for a fall.

The key in golf is to keep your channels open so your brain can gather the information necessary to locate the cup and figure out how to get the ball to the bottom of it. Once the information starts to flow, all you need to do is stand back and let the process run itself.

To demonstrate how perfectly your systems work, stand a few feet away and toss a ball to a friend. Watch how he tracks the object in time and space and how his arm comes up at just the right time to catch the ball. Like the Major League center fielder described earlier, his tracking systems are working just fine. Toss the ball back and forth a few times, each time moving farther away from your friend. You'll notice that he automatically calculates your new position, as well as the additional force necessary to toss you the ball, without even thinking about it. Then ask him to close his eyes and then toss him the ball. Be careful, though, because once he shuts down his tracking system, he won't be able to catch the ball as he did just a minute ago, so don't throw it directly at him or you'll bean him.

Unwittingly, many golfers shut down their tracking systems, systems you need to have in good working order to play your best golf. They don't actually close their eyes, but they do clog their channels in other ways. They think about things that have nothing to do with gathering information for the shot at hand, like a three-putt on the last hole or that triple bogey that ruined their score. You can't focus on the present when you're stranded in the past.

Strange as it may seem, in a game where hitting the target is all that matters, many golfers hardly give the target a glance. They're so concerned with swing mechanics and/or the trouble protecting the target that their mental screen has no room for the target.

Then there is the player who blocks his automatic tracking systems by focusing almost exclusively on the wrong target—the ball. Have you ever wondered why so many golfers can take beautiful practice swings when they're hitting dandelions, but look distinctly different when they're swinging at a golf ball? That's because they've made the ball their target, to the exclusion of the actual target. They've gathered plenty of information on where the ball is, but not much on where the target is. Their muscles are ball bound instead of target bound. In effect, they've made a plan based on a target they know nothing about. It's something they wouldn't dream of doing in any other target sport—not in darts or horseshoes, not even in pitching pennies.

BE TARGET BOUND

When you play darts or toss a horseshoe, where is your focus? How about when you're shooting a jump shot, or pointing the remote to change the channel on your TV? The answer is the target. You don't think about the angle of your elbow or when to release the dart—if you did, you might miss the wall, never mind the dartboard! But most golfers don't focus on the target when they play golf. Instead of relinquishing to their subconscious the mechanics of getting the ball from point A to point B, they're still thinking about their swing as they stare at the ball.

Hitting a golf ball to a target is a lot like pitching pennies, that game we played as kids where the one who tossed the penny closest to the wall won. You put your toes on the line, looked at the target, and your brain automatically figured out how far it was, how hard to swing your arm, and when to release the penny. In golf, the same thing happens when you stand behind the ball with your senses wide open. You are relying on your unconscious competence to make the calculations for you. For every shot, get a case of the "eyes" not the "I's."

Now that you know *where you're going,* the second part of your plan deals with *how to get there,* but first you must decide exactly what game you're playing.

FIRST DECIDE WHAT GAME YOU'RE PLAYING

There are two kinds of golf: Spectacular Golf and Scoring Golf. The object of Spectacular Golf is to hit heroic shots by firing at every flag, pounding driver off every par-4 and par-5, and attacking the course regardless of the consequences. The only strategy is attack. You don't keep score because you expect sensational shots and daring recoveries, sprinkled with disasters. It's a good game, if you understand its evaluation system: spectacular results.

You announce Spectacular Golf on the 1st tee and you prepare yourself so that bad breaks, high scores, and lost balls don't upset you. They are as much a part of Spectacular Golf as getting wet is a part of swimming. This is a fun game to play as long as you don't run out of balls, but it is not Scoring Golf.

Unfortunately, most golfers play Spectacular Golf without realizing it. They mix the crash-and-burn strategies of Spectacular Golf with the evaluation system of Scoring Golf. When their score card ends up with more Xs than a bowling sheet, they berate themselves for their lack of talent. Though it's a popular game, this book is not about Spectacular Golf; it's about Scoring Golf.

SCORING GOLF

If you want to succeed at Scoring Golf, you need to use both the strategies and an evaluation system germane to that game. That means you must dissociate yourself from the principles of Spectacular Golf. Scoring Golf is a game of strategy. Your shot selection is based on your current on-course ability, the conditions (wind, pin positions, hazard locations, rain, etc.) and the circumstances of play: Is it match or medal, early or late in the round? Is your opponent in the weeds or next to the pin?

Scoring Golf is a game of position. As you progress from the tee, where by rule, all positions are equal, you either increase or decrease your positional advantage until you hole out—the ultimate positional advantage. A great player develops a plan and maneuvers the ball to favorable positions around the course, just as the good billiards player controls the cue ball to run the table. Thus there is only one strategy for Scoring Golf—POSITION—and those who consistently gain positional advantage consistently score well.

Positional Advantage

Like your swing concept, your golf game will never be any better than your concept of what a good golf game should be! If your concept of the game is hitting pretty shots, having fun, gaining respect, or hitting it farther than the next guy, then you'll focus all your energies toward that goal and scoring will become an afterthought.

You may not even be aware that you're doing this and, if somebody asked you, you'd say that score is most important, but subconsciously your priorities drive your behavior. Scorers prioritize for low scores and use the swing as a vehicle. How the shot affects their position is the important factor for scoring. This way they keep a clear mind that can focus on their most important goal—scoring.

YOUR MOST IMPORTANT CHOICE OF THE ROUND
Your Strength and Weakness Profile can help you choose the correct tees, which is the most important decision you can make for the well-being and improvement of your game.

No matter how challenging they are, great golf courses are also fair. Long par-4s generally feature larger greens than the shorter par-4s on the course. A large green provides more room for error for a longer approach shot and more surface area on which to stop a lower-trajectory shot. The shorter par-4 usually features smaller greens surrounded by trouble and a high-trajectory shot is required to stop the ball quickly.

If you play the course from too long a distance, the course is more difficult than the architect intended it to be. By doing this, you'll turn most of your strengths into weaknesses and, therefore, be unable to fit your Strength and Weakness Profile to the defenses set up by the architect. When you play from the wrong tees, in effect you surrender your strengths, expose your weaknesses, and set yourself up for a flood of No signals that will simply ruin your game.

PRACTICAL ASPECTS OF GOOD PLAN-MAKING

The Master Plan

Playing one shot at a time is poor advice and not the way a champion plays. Every shot plan fits the master plan you develop before your round. Your game is a tapestry of individual shot plans wrapped in overall strategy accumulated over hundreds of rounds.

Ben Hogan was famous for developing a game plan so detailed that it included where he would hit each shot and what club he would use to hit that shot. Legend has it that when a reporter asked Hogan if he was making any special adjustments for the 1950 U.S. Open at Merion Golf Club, Hogan said he was taking his seven-iron out of his bag. When the reporter asked why, Hogan replied, "Because there are no seven-iron shots at Merion." True or not—Hogan liked to play head games with both the press and his opponents—it highlights the need for a master game plan supported by each individual shot plan as your round develops. The master plan is your blueprint; the individual plans are your series of adjustments.

The complexity of your master plan will vary depending on your level of play. A high-handicap golfer who slices the ball should have a simple master plan, for instance, making sure he aims correctly to allow for the slice and hitting a five-wood off the tee when there's trouble on the right. For the low-handicap tournament player, the master plan might involve a practice round where he charts every yardage and every club. In any case, while you must be free to make adjustments based on changing circumstances and conditions, the individual shot plans coordinate with the hue of the master plan.

Individual Shot Plans

The first step in making a shot plan is to evaluate the psychological momentum of your round. Reading this factor correctly will dramatically increase your consistency. Always develop your plan with the following questions in mind: How does the success or failure of your shot plan affect your momentum? Is the risk worth the reward? Rate your current momentum. Are you on an even keel, purring along, carrying out your master plan? Or has a wave of successes carried you away from your plan and left you thinking that you can do anything you want to with the golf ball?

Cumulative Reward—Be Careful with Momentum

While players feed off momentum—those cumulative rewards where success builds on success, and one great shot inspires another—it can contain the seeds of collapse if it distracts you from your plan. Flush with success, and flooded with adrenaline, there is a bulletproof feeling that often captures a golfer whose momentum is in high gear. Like the gambler on a hot streak, their shot plans become increasingly aggressive until the inevitable occurs and they're captured by the architect's defenses.

When you're playing exceptionally well, don't be tempted into taking unnecessary or foolish chances. Hitting your driver on a narrow hole when your master plan called for a two-iron, or firing at a pin tucked behind a pond when you should have played to the fat part of the green, can stop your momentum in a hurry.

Are You Listening to the Wrong CD?

The flip side of success leading to failure is the more common syndrome of "cumulative disreward" (CD). As your round progresses, you make a bunch of good swings but nothing works out, and your best efforts go unrewarded. CD usually strikes around the 14th hole of an otherwise so-so round. It causes those head-shaking, after-round autopsies that start with "I was playing okay until 14, when suddenly the roof caved in."

Actually, it wasn't sudden; it was incremental. You *were* swinging well, and making decent plans, but the rub of the green had it out for you that day. You made a great swing on the 2nd hole, but the ball buried in the lip of the bunker thanks to a random gust of wind (disreward 1). On the 6th hole, you rolled a seemingly perfect 10-footer that circled the inner edge of the cup before it lipped out—there was no way it could stay out—but it did (disreward 2). On the 8th hole, you hit it pure off the tee, but the ball hit a sprinkler head in the middle of the fairway and kicked into the rough (disreward 3). By the 14th hole, with disrewards stacking up, your brain starts to get the idea that no matter how well you play, it isn't good enough.

So, you decide to make something happen. You attack a pin you should avoid and, though you hit a solid shot, you come up a few yards short and the ball rolls down the shaved bank and into the greenside water hazard. At this point, a full-blown case of CD kicks in and you quit—you stop trying. The statement "It's not my day" usually accompanies the CDs and if you think it isn't, it isn't.

Rumpelstiltskin Solution

In the Grimm's fairy tale "Rumpelstiltskin," the greedy king orders the beautiful maiden to spin flax into gold. The maiden promises the evil dwarf her firstborn if he will help her, which he does. The dwarf tells her that he won't hold her to her promise if she can guess his name. She does, and Rumpelstiltskin, furious, destroys himself.

It is the same with cumulative disreward. You can combat it by being able to name it (recognize it) each time it appears. If you label each disreward accurately, the insidious process never takes hold of you.

What Score Do You Need?

The next factor in your plan is figuring what score you need and what score you can't survive. Determine where you have to position the ball to make the score you need, and eliminate the area that produces big numbers. When brain-runner extraordinaire Ben Hogan was asked why he didn't go for a certain par-5 in two, from a distance he could have easily covered, his curt reply was, "Because I didn't need a three."

Following are examples of how to factor into your plan the score you need versus the score you can't survive.

WHAT SCORE DO YOU NEED?

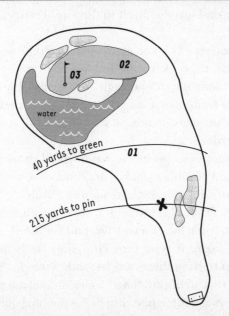

It's a par-5 and you've driven the ball to position X, an ideal position in the fairway. You have 215 yards to a pin that is closely guarded by a water hazard. In order to make a good plan, first take into consideration the circumstances of play. The example assumes a lie good enough to play each option and a Strength and Weakness Profile that indicates you have the on-course ability to play each option. The bail-out area is short right; the trouble is straight ahead in the form of water in front, and bunkers behind the green.

Circumstance 1: It's the 2nd hole of a thirty-six-hole medal play tournament and you're even par.

Option 1: Lay up to 40 yards, which probably means you'll make par (you wedge it on the green and two-putt). Of course, that depends on your wedge play strength, which should be clearly defined in your Strength and Weakness Profile. If your wedge play is exceptional, then birdie four becomes a solid possibility in this scenario. The outcome for this plan, if successful, is par, possible birdie. If you mishit your wedge shot, and leave yourself in three-putt range, bogey six is also possible.

Option 2: From 215, you go for the fingerlike portion of the green to the right with your five-wood. If you're successful, you'll face a long putt for an eagle. You'll probably two-putt for a birdie, but from such a long distance, a three-putt is also possible. The outcome for this plan, if successful, is definite par probable birdie.

If your shot ends up in the water, you'll drop close to the green. It's still possible to make par, with a close wedge shot and one-putt, but a two-putt for bogey is more likely.

Option 3: From 215, you go for the flag with a three-iron. If you make it, you'll have an easy two-putt for birdie and perhaps a one-putt eagle. If your three-iron shot lands in the water, though, you're lying three and left with a tough 120-yard shot over water to a tight pin. Since you absolutely must clear the water, you bring a three-putt into play—double bogey—by landing well past the pin. Worse yet, you might find the back bunker and bring an even bigger number into play. If you can't afford a double bogey or worse, this is the wrong plan.

Though these are not the only scenarios, they are the most likely. Whatever scenario you come up with, the bottom line is what score do you need to make and what score can't you survive? If you make a lot of birdies per round, and you've determined you're facing a strong field, you might give Option 3 a try since it's only the second hole of a thirty-six-hole event. Granted you'd have to play your best, but you can survive a triple bogey if you make six birdies over the next thirty-four holes. However, if you're not a big birdie producer and the field is mediocre, then Option 1 is your strongest plan.

KNOW THE COMPETITION

An essential element of superior planning is knowing how you rate in relationship to the field you're playing against. For example, when the wind blows, a lot of players feel they're losing ground if they make a couple of bogies. They start to press and shoot themselves out of the tournament. The player who can read the field knows that a strong wind raises the effective eighteen-hole par. An expert at planning and evaluation understands that when the wind is blowing 20 mph, par 72 becomes more like par 75. This prevents them from making bad plans in the wind in an attempt to stay even with par 72.

When you change the circumstances, you change the planning requirements. If the scenario above occurred on the last hole where you're one down and your opponent is already on the green in two shots, the circumstances dictate that you go with Option 3. If, however, your opponent is lying two in the water, Option 1 is your strongest plan.

As part of the 30-Second Swing, make it a habit to ask yourself, "What score do I need and what score can't I survive?" When you do, you can allow the circumstances to shape your plan. Champions consider the circumstances of play for every shot; good players do it most of the time, and the rest of the golf population rarely considers the circumstances. This lack of proper planning is a major barrier to lowering your handicap and winning more matches and tournaments.

The Conditions of Play

Now let's look at an example of how you factor the conditions of play into your plan. As always, to do this effectively you need an accurate strength and weakness profile. In this example, you're playing a dogleg to the left where a 10-mph wind is blowing from left to right.

THE CONDITIONS OF PLAY

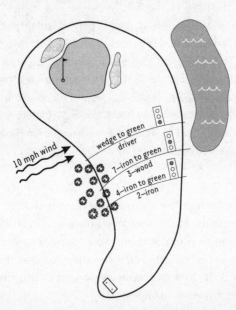

Option 1: Hit your driver to position X, leaving you a pitching wedge to the pin, which would create a green light situation—go for the flag.

Option 2: Hit a three-wood from the tee to avoid the water on the right. But this leaves a seven-iron to the green, creating a yellow light situation—proceed with caution.

Option 3: Hit a two-iron from the tee to take the water on the right completely out of play. But this leaves you a four-iron into the green and a red light situation (don't go), which is one you want to avoid creating if possible.

PLANNING'S QUID PRO QUO

Sometimes when you play too safe with one shot, you set yourself up for an extremely difficult and dangerous next shot, which is why no great player ever played one shot at a time. For example, if you're too cautious off the tee and hit with a two-iron when you should have only dropped down to a three-wood, you effectively change the hole's degree of difficulty. You're left with a long-iron to a green designed to accept a mid-size.

If you're aggressive on the front end of your plan, and you're successful, unless conditions/circumstances suddenly change, make sure you follow it by being aggressive on the back end. Otherwise, you won't be able to cash in on the gamble you took on the front end. In the same sense, it's foolish to play safe and then, on a whim, go for broke.

A Tee Shot Quiz

When planning your tee shot, you should ask yourself these kinds of questions.

Can I clear those trees with a driver?

If I slice my tee shot, will it reach the water?

What other clubs in my bag have a chance of reaching the water?

How much better am I with the wedge than the seven-iron?

Am I much more accurate with a seven-iron than a five-iron?

Am I more skilled with a three-wood than a two-iron?

You'll know the answers if you keep your statistics.

It won't do you much good to hit a driver inside 100 yards if you're not a good wedge player and it doesn't make sense to hit a two-iron to play safe if your two-iron is a troublesome club.

When you're planning a shot, go through the following mental checklist. At first, the process will take some extra time but, before long, it will become so instinctual that you'll do it unconsciously in a matter of seconds.

Club Selection

Know how far you hit each club. There is approximately a 4-degree loft difference between each of your irons and each degree represents about two and a half yards' difference in distance, which means that there is about 10 yards' difference between each club. So, if you know your average eight-iron distance, and then add or subtract 10 yards, you can calculate the distance for the rest of your irons. For example, if eight-iron = 140 yards, then seven-iron = 150 yards, and nine-iron = 130 yards. Check your long irons: if you have a slow swing speed, you may hit all your long irons about the same distance and you should replace them with high-lofted utility woods.

THE CONDITIONS OF PLAY

Reading Your Lie

In the rough, when the grass is against you—growing away from the target—you'll need to swing harder on pitch shots and add at least one club for long shots. When the grass is growing toward the target—a flier lie—you'll need to swing easier around the greens and take at least one less club for full shots from the fairway rough.

Neutralize the Wind

If the wind is greater than 5 miles per hour, it will affect your shot. If the wind is less than 5 miles per hour, ignore it. To evaluate the wind, check the direction and speed of the clouds, how the flag is responding, and, most important, the movement of the treetops, which is where the wind will have the most effect on the ball. A side wind slows the ball up and magnifies its spin and, when the ball reaches its apex, the wind can blow the ball sideways. Thus, a side wind is usually not a helping wind.

In any case, solid contact is the key to keeping the ball on line in the wind. Most golfers however do just the opposite—they overswing and mishit the ball, leaving it at the mercy of the wind. Grip down, swing smoothly, and take more club, but unless you're an expert, avoid swing changes that can lead to poor contact, like moving the ball back in your stance or trying to punch the ball with an abbreviated swing. Basically, the conditions are tough enough without you suddenly changing your swing!

Addition/Subtraction

Once you've established the distance to the center of the green, determine the relationship of the pin to the center of the green. Most greens are at least 30 yards deep—a three-club range. If the pin is in the back of the green, you need to add about 10 yards to your calculation; if it's in the front of the green, you need to subtract about 10 yards. You also need to adjust for the elevation: for every 30 feet (10 yards) of elevation, add (uphill) or subtract (downhill) a club.

Never-Never Land

1. Never try a shot on the course that you haven't practiced, and hit well on the driving range. If you're considering a two-iron from the rough over a lake to an elevated green and you haven't practiced that shot, then you have the wrong plan.

2. Never make the mistake of having to play two trouble shots in a row. Get out of trouble the first time. Remember: *safe* means *safe.*

3. Never fall asleep on your layup shot. Give it the same attention and planning as any other shot.

   a. Never lay up too long. The smooth, easy swing that usually accompanies a layup shot often contacts the ball so solidly that it flies a club longer than normal. Being 15 yards short of the hazard is not much different than being 20 yards short, but one yard too long is a penalty, so choose your club conservatively.

   b. Never lay up to an uneven lie. As a rule, it's better to hit a seven-iron from an even lie than a nine-iron when the ball is below your feet.

   c. Never lay up to an awkward distance. Even great players sometimes have trouble when they're at a distance that's between clubs. For example, it's too far for a normal eight-iron, but a bit too close for a seven-iron. Say your normal sand wedge flies 80 yards and you have 230 yards to the pin. Choose the layup club that goes 150 yards so you can hit a full sand wedge to the green, rather than a tricky half-wedge shot.

HARD OR EASY? WHAT TO DO WHEN YOU'RE BETWEEN CLUBS

Let's say your normal nine-iron is 125 yards and you have 130 yards to the pin. What club do you choose? These "tweeners" are never easy: it's too far for your nine-iron but too short for your eight-iron. There's also the danger that, because you're unsure of what club to hit, you'll make a bad swing. Remember, a bad swing with the right club results in just as poor a shot as a good swing with the wrong club. As long as you're unsure about which club to hit, you really don't have much of a chance to produce a good shot.

If your tweeners have a history of ending up in trouble, here's the solution. If you're a fast-swinging power hitter, take one less club and hit it harder (in this case, the nine-iron). If you're a smooth swinger with a syrupy action, take one club more and hit it easy. When you match your club selection to your swing tempo, you'll never have to violate your internal metronome, the personal gauge that sets your natural swing pace. Abiding by your internal rhythm will put you at ease and you'll be able to handle those awkward distances without a problem.

4. Never aim where a straight ball will put you in trouble. Aiming at the trouble and trying to curve the ball away from it is a bad plan that often ends in disaster. No matter how consistent your fade or draw, aiming a ball into a lake and expecting the spin to carry the ball to safety subjects you to the ever-present Murphy's Law. Sure enough, you'll make your best swing of the day and hit it dead straight—into the water.

5. Never miss a green on the short side. For a pin tucked near the edge of a green, steer clear of the green's short side—the area where you'll have a small amount of green to work with if you have to get up and down.

6. Never swing hard in the wind. Downwind the ball goes farther than you think; into wind it balloons; and crosswinds (of the same direction) increase sidespin. Sometimes a wind behind your back, especially over water, causes the ball to drop out of the sky suddenly and it falls short of the target because it never reached its normal trajectory.

7. Never leave yourself a downwind bunker shot or pitch shot to a tucked pin. It's easy to be too aggressive going after a

pin into the wind. If you hit the ball too far, you'll leave yourself a shot that's tough to stop coming back because the downwind takes the spin off the ball.

8. All 3 footers are not equal. When chipping, pitching, or approach putting, never leave yourself a sidehill putt. Always try to leave the ball below the hole so you're putting straight back up the slope.

9. Never play through a No signal. Step back and change the No to a Go signal using the techniques outlined in the next chapter.

10. Never play a shot for which you have no exact destination. The most important part of your plan is picking a target. The fairway or the green is not specific enough. Your target must be clear, distinct, and as specific as you can make it: for example, the left center of the fairway, in line with the lower left branches of the large tree in the distance, and across from the far edge of the fairway bunker on the right.

11. Never make a swing unless you're mentally engaged and physically relaxed.

12. Never quit.

13. Never think the game owes you anything.

14. Never make a swing without the full routine of your 30-Second Swing.

EASY AS 1,2,3 AND A,B,C

In evaluating each shot, use the 1, 2, 3/A, B, C coding system to rate the demands of each component. First, rate the target's position. Rate easy-to-hit fairways and unprotected pins as 1 for GO or attack. These are green light situations where Go signals come easily.

Use 2 for a target whose position requires more caution (yellow light). Rate difficult driving holes and protected pin placements 3 for NO or play safe (red light).

ΣASY AS 1, 2, 3

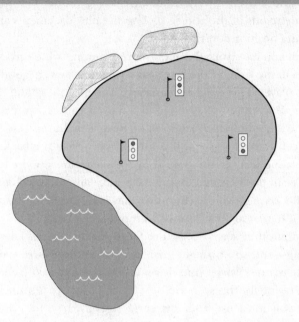

How you rate the shot also depends on how you're playing. Rate your overall game: A, when you're firing on all cylinders; B, when you're playing your average; and C, when your swing has deserted you and you can barely scrape it around.

This is a strictly personalized and subjective system. If you tried to play Tiger Woods's game, without his Strength and Weakness Profile, you'd run out of balls before you finished nine holes. Therefore, it does no good to sprinkle your playing résumé with puffery; in fact, it does great harm. If you once hit a five-iron onto a green 200 yards away and you delude yourself into thinking that that's how far you always hit your five, you are only fooling yourself. This is why digital record keeping is so vital. In the cold light of the statistics, it's hard to fool yourself.

Your final rating is the club you've selected. Label it 1 if it's a strength; 2 if it's a moderate strength, and 3 if it's a weakness.

Obviously, making a plan for each shot involves having an accurate and current Strength and Weakness Profile that matches the demands of the course such as the pin placements and key driving positions off the tee.

Say you have your B game. You're planning a 110-yard shot to a pin in the front of the green, and you're not a very good short-iron player. This is a 2-B-2 situation. The general guideline is to treat all front pin placements as 2 flags because, if you're short of the flag, you're probably not on the green. In this case, aim at the center of the green. If you nail it, you're at the back of the green and you can two-putt. If you're a little short of the middle, you're in birdie range. In this example, your coding changes to a 2-B-1 rating if you're short-iron play is strong. With this rating, you'd have good justification to shoot at the pin.

In another scenario, you're faced with a narrow fairway—3 rating—and you brought your C game to the course today. To make matters worse, your driver is one of your weakest clubs—3. The rating for this scenario is 3-C-3. Unless there is some reason why you must use your driver (a forced carry, for instance), change to a plan that rates 3-C-1. Use a 1 club—a five-wood or even a five-iron—just to keep the ball in play. When the course gives you a 3 target, only attack when you have your A game and a 1 club. If you violate this guideline, you'll pay the price sooner rather than later.

Keep in mind that the rating you apply to each situation depends on your current, up-to-the-minute talent level. If you're not a very accurate iron player, and the pin is tucked just beyond a water hazard, steer clear of it. If you're normally a straight driver but find you're struggling with the big stick that day, hit a three- or five-wood from the tee.

THREES AND C'S

It sounds complicated if you've never done this kind of planning for each shot, but once you make it part of your 30-Second Swing, it becomes automatic so you don't have to think about it. To get started, replay your rounds after you finish, labeling each shot to see how good your plan making is. If you're coming up with a lot of 3s and Cs as in 3-C-3, the plan segment of your 30-Second Swing needs work.

The ultimate is to produce all 1-A-1 plans, which would promote a state of perfect permission and a "flow of Go" known as the Zone. Though this is the goal of your practice and effort, it is seldom achieved for more than a few shots a round. Still, the better your shot plans, the better your outcomes, so make sure all the elements of a good plan are part of every shot you play.

A PUTTING ROUTINE: SO THAT'S WHAT IT'S FOR

You should apply the principles of the 30-Second Swing to every shot including your short game. But, while containing all the basics of your 30-Second Swing, your routine is a little different for putting because it involves triangulation where you look at your putt from three vantage points that form the points of a triangle. If you use just one position to determine the location of an object, you risk parallax—distortion via the position of the observer. That's why surveyors use more than one position to measure the exact location of objects—they can't afford to be fooled and neither can you. Here's how it works.

Use the three positions on the triangle—behind the hole, behind the ball, and midway between the ball and the hole on the low side of the slope—to accurately determine the speed and break of your putt. As you move from point to point on the triangle, your commitment to the line of the putt often changes. This is as it should be because, as you gather more information from different vantage points, your brain adjusts the line or curve of the putt automatically. Your brain needs to keep changing its mind until it measures the distance and slope accurately. All you have to do is pay attention—don't gaze off in the distance or think about the last drive you hit into the woods—and your brain will track the target.

Just as with your full swing, when you go behind the ball, you make a final commitment that will stay with you through your stroke. When you're fully committed to the line and the speed, you'll receive your Go signal. With your tracking system locked on the target, proceed directly to the ball and let your instincts make the putt.

SUMMARY: THE ELEMENTS OF A GOOD PLAN

Know where your momentum is leading you.

Know your distance to the target.

Know how far you hit each of your clubs.

Know what score you need.

Know what score you can't survive.

Know the circumstances.

Know the conditions.

Know your shot shape (the spin and trajectory of the shot you choose).

Know where the trouble is.

Know where the bail-out area is.

Know your current Strength and Weakness Profile.

Having gathered all the necessary information and made the appropriate evaluations, you're standing behind the ball with a detailed map to your target. Your shot plan dictates not only where the ball is going, but how it's going to get there. You've planned for the spin (left to right, straight, or right to left) and the trajectory (high, medium, or low) that will get the job done. You are now ready to summon the relaxation response, image the shot in full detail, and, with the support of full commitment, address the ball in an avalanche of Go—all of which you'll learn in the following chapters.

CHAPTER 5

Golf in the Go Lane

Golf is first a game of seeing and feeling. It can teach you stillness of mind and a sensitivity to the textures of wind and green. The best instructional books have always said this. Golf is also a game to teach you about the messages from within, about the subtle voice of the body-mind. And once you understand them you can more clearly see your "hamartia," the ways in which your approach to the game reflects your entire life.

—MICHAEL MURPHY, *Golf in the Kingdom*

INTERNAL MESSAGES

IN MY players school I often ask my students: Did you receive any messages this morning? Most shake their heads no. Then I ask some other questions designed to show them that they all received messages, though they didn't recognize them as such.

Did anyone eat breakfast this morning? Almost all nod their heads yes. Did anyone go to the bathroom? They smile and shift in their chairs. Did anyone fall asleep last night; did anyone turn on the air conditioner in their room or take a drink of water yesterday during your round?

If you're like my students, and every other human being on the planet, you answered yes to many of these questions. But how did you know it was time to do all these things? The answer is that your body sends you a steady stream of messages. Some messages are reminders (it's time to eat), some of them warnings (that's hot!), some of them encouraging (go ahead, you can do it) and some are caveats (be careful with this one). Fortunately your brain is in constant communication with you.

Thus, in addition to external messages that bombard you, there are internal messages sent from your subconscious. The term *subconscious* refers to all of your experience that is not currently in your conscious mind. All your emotions, beliefs, memories, and skills are stored in your subconscious. It contains all your can-dos, such as being able to play a bunker shot, and all your can't-dos, perhaps those slippery sidehill three-footers. It's all there in your subconscious, waiting to be of service.

And what a wonderful messenger service it is! It helps you make the right business decisions, choose the right friends, and marry the right person. It is commonly known as going with your gut feeling, but it doesn't come from your stomach, it comes from your subconscious. Your subconscious communicates in signals and, to play your best golf, you must recognize what these signals are trying to tell you. You may feel unsure or decisive, uneasy or calm, worried or confident, distressed or relaxed, annoyed or serene. These messages, first identified by Chuck Hogan, are No and Go signals, and this chapter will help you recognize even the most subtle No signals and provide you with the techniques to turn them into Go signals.

THE RINGMASTER OF NO/GO SIGNALS:
THE FRONTAL LOBE

Is there a specific part of the brain where the No/Go system is located—a ringmaster that coordinates all the acts that combine to make us human? No one knows for sure, but a leading candidate is the frontal lobe.

Some of the best clues to how the normal brain operates come from studying the results of injuries to various locations in the brain. One of the most famous studies is related in Antonio Damasio's best-selling book *Descartes' Error.* In 1848, Phineas T. Gage, a railway worker, suffered a horrific injury when an explosion sent an iron rod slicing through the frontal lobe of his brain. Miraculously, Gage, a kind and well-liked person before the accident, regained his health and well-being, with only one major exception. After the injury, Gage's personality changed so dramatically that, as his close friends said, "Gage was no longer Gage." He went from friendly and helpful to angry and quarrelsome; a person who was once reliable, trustworthy, and socially gracious became unreliable, vulgar, and an altogether belligerent man with nothing to be belligerent about.

"Why is this sad story worth telling?" asks Dr. Damasio, and he answers his own question: "The answer is simple. . . . Gage's story hinted at an amazing fact: Somehow there were systems in the human brain dedicated more to reasoning than to anything else and in particular to the personal and social dimensions of reasoning. The observance of previously acquired social convention and ethical rules could be lost because of brain damage even when neither basic intellect nor language seemed compromised." For Gage, the normal system of checks and balances, the finely tuned No/Go system that allows us to make our way through this world, was shredded. But this was just one early case. Since then, a bulk of research supports the fact that, as

Damasio's inference about the Gage case suggested, "something in the brain was concerned specifically with unique human properties, among them the ability to anticipate the future and plan accordingly."

According to Jeffrey Schwartz, a research scientist at UCLA School of Medicine, PET scans show that the underside of the brain's prefrontal lobe is overactive in obsessive-compulsive disorder (OCD). In fact, when the warning system located in your frontal lobe is down, all sorts of problems occur, far more serious than the kind you face on the golf course. There is a checker in your brain whose job it is to give a final okay to whatever it is you're about to do. Schwartz thinks that the alarm can become stuck and send out a continuous bogus message that something is wrong, placing the individual in a perpetual and paralyzing state of No.

When a person is healthy, the ringmaster of No/Go in your frontal lobe screens out these bogus warnings. However, when the frontal lobe is injured, the person can be afflicted by "tyrannical obsessions," as Schwartz calls them. Let's say that just before you leave the house you think, "Did I turn the iron off?" which is a valuable No signal that helps you avoid starting a fire. Your ringmaster tells you that you did turn it off and away you go. If you're an obsessive-compulsive, however, you keep receiving the No signal. In this case, you can't generate permission to leave the house because you have to keep checking to make sure the iron is off. When your warning system is stuck on No, it becomes almost impossible to function as your internal world boomerangs back on itself in a reverberating circuit of Nos. The opposite occurs when the checker is for some reason obliterated. Absent a censor, antisocial behavior can result, ranging in severity from unpleasant to sociopathic.

Obviously the health of our internal message system is important to the quality of life we lead, and by understanding how this message system works, we can improve all aspects of our life, including golf.

GOLF IN A STATE OF NO

Unfortunately, if you're like most golfers, you receive No signals when you play, but you ignore them. In doing so, you're ignoring warnings from your brain and in effect you're playing against yourself. It's an exhausting way to play the game because you fight yourself internally, which is one battle you'll never win.

The feeling produced by playing golf in a state of No, where you're inundated by No signals, varies from person to person, but it's basically an anxious feeling about the shot at hand. The state of No often features a high-pitched internal voice that bombards you with negative ideas and belittles your golf skills. George Plimpton described it best when he recounted his feelings playing in a pro-am in front of 3,000 people. All he could hear as he stood over the ball was "Chinese admirals shouting swing instructions." Your admirals may be shouting in another language but, no matter the dialect, when you doubt your plan or you're confused about the shot you're about to play, you're sure to receive a No signal.

In essence, by ignoring these No signals, you're violating your internal system of checks and balances. This sophisticated system is the product of millions of years of evolution, where the impetuous conscious mind wants to act, and the wise subconscious methodically verifies whether the action is appropriate.

Learning to decode these signals—to recognize No signals and convert them into Go signals—is the most effective way of taking control of your golf game. Once you can do this you'll have the ability to create a steady stream of Go signals on the golf course, a powerful current that carries you into a state of Go, often called the Zone. Golf in a state of Go is a high-performance mode where you turn your golf swing over to unconscious competence, take your hands off the steering wheel, and go along for the ride.

PERMISSION

In describing concepts in this chapter, I follow Chuck Hogan's conceptual base and use *mind* and *brain* interchangeably since they are intimately related, albeit in ways not yet fully understood. One way to look at it is that the mind is what the brain does for a living.

For purposes of discussion, I have divided the mind into the conscious and the subconscious mind. As part of my academic training I dissected a cadaver, and when I arrived at the brain there was, I can assure you, nothing marked conscious and subconscious—but it's still a helpful distinction.

Your conscious mind is represented by whatever image is on your mental screen. Here, images appear one at a time, although they move in microseconds. The conscious mind is short-term and impulsive. It's puerile, a youngster that says, "Let's go do it! Let's go hit that two-iron up over those trees, into the wind, 210 yards over water!"

Fortunately, we have a vast pool of knowledge in our subconscious comprised of all our experience. The subconscious judges what the conscious mind wants to do and decides if it is appropriate. It searches your database for similar experiences in order to decide whether to veto or endorse the plan. If you have the skills and the correct plan, you'll receive a Go signal. If you don't have the skill, or your plan is dangerously flawed, you'll receive a No signal. When the conscious mind says, "Let's do it," and the subconscious says, "I've checked it out—go ahead," the congruence between the two gives you permission, and permission is the key to success.

Permission focuses your brain on whatever you are about to

CHAMPION'S FLOW OF GO

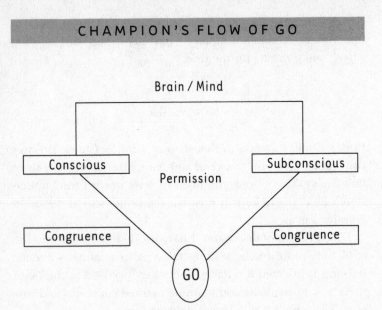

do, coordinating your body's systems (balance, vision, muscula-ture, hormones, blood pressure, etc.) so they are dedicated to accomplishing the task. This is what I mean by focusing your brain—you bring to bear all of your resources to accomplish the chosen objective. The image agenda—whatever is on your men-tal screen—receives top priority once permission is granted. Having permission doesn't mean you will be successful every time—you may mishit that two-iron—but permission does give you the best chance for success. You can be sure that if you play in a state of perfect permission on every golf shot, you will play the best golf you are capable of playing.

Creating Permission

The key to creating permission is selecting a plan that will receive the stamp of approval from your subconscious. Other factors also contribute to gaining permission in the form of your Go signal. In Chapter 9, you'll learn that it's far easier to play in a flow of Go signals when your brain is stocked with past successes, what I call Tracks of Excellence. Past success is the foundation of confidence. If you've hit many a good six-iron over water into a side wind, then those Tracks of Excellence help you to imagine that you can do it again when the time comes for the next six-iron.

Preparation

Another way to ensure that you receive permission is preparation. When it comes to hitting a golf shot, the only element that you have 100 percent control over is the preparation phase, that is, what you do before you set the club in motion. The preparation phase extends all the way back to your practice regimen where, having identified your weaknesses from your stat keeping, you work to turn them into strengths. The progression is straightforward: the more strengths you have, the better plans you can devise; the more your plans are based on strengths, the more permission you generate; the more permission, the greater the flow of Go signals.

Legend has it that a golfer, on his way to the 1st tee, drove past Gary Player practicing his bunker play. When the golfer finished his round four and a half hours later, he drove past the same bunker and Player was still there practicing. Gary Player is perhaps the best bunker player the game has ever seen. How much permission do you think he receives when his plan calls for a sand shot? Lee Trevino is no slouch either when it comes to bunker play, but early in his career, by his own admission, his bunker skills were horrible. "When I first came on the tour I was the worst bunker player you ever saw," said Trevino, "I was sculling 'em and hitting chunkers—it got so bad that finally I said to my caddie, 'Who's the best bunker player out here? I need help.'" Trevino paid a visit to Gary Player, and in doing so converted a weakness into strength. It has been said that luck is when preparation meets opportunity; maybe that's why the champions are so lucky.

Creating Can-Do Situations

The third way to generate permission is to focus on the characteristics of the target to the exclusion of all else. As you have seen, golf is a target game, and your brain requires information about the target's location so it can direct your muscles to move the club on the correct path and at just the right speed. You need to become a receiving station for information about the target, with your mind collecting data about the wind, the yardage, the location of the hazards, etc. When you have enough information, and your plan complements your Strength and Weakness Profile, you've created a can-do situation where your subconscious reviews your plan, finds everything in order, and gives you the go-ahead to execute the shot.

Perception: They Just Seem Big

How you see yourself in relation to others can affect the way you perform. When weekend golfers have the opportunity to stand side by side with golfing superstars like Jack Nicklaus or Arnold Palmer at a Tour event, they're often surprised at how normal their idols are in size. This is because of the natural tendency to build heroes into larger-than-life characters in the mind's eye. Tour veteran Andrew Magee said that the first time he played with Greg Norman, he expected the Shark to be eight feet tall and five feet wide.

How we perceive an opponent, or a situation, influences how we perform against that opponent or in that situation. Grant Waite recounted the first time he played with Nicklaus. On the 1st tee, Waite's introduction took all of ten seconds, as the starter mentioned Waite's lone Tour win. But the Bear's introduction seemed to last an eternity, with the starter mentioning each and every one of Nicklaus's major championships. "By the time he was finished," said Waite, "I felt like I was two feet tall." Unfortunately, that's just how he played that round—like he was two feet tall.

The perceptions of reality that you create in your brain are just that—your perceptions. You've have a choice: in your mind's eye, you can make your opponent bigger or smaller, stronger or weaker, invincible (in which case you'll probably lose) or vulnerable (in which case you'll have a chance to win). To play golf to the best of your ability, you must become adept at running your own brain. If you don't, there are plenty of people ready to run it for you. Everyone has strengths and weaknesses, but we generally overestimate our opponent's strengths and underestimate his weaknesses. Unfortunately, we often do the reverse with our own games; we underestimate our strengths and exaggerate our weaknesses.

The next time you face a skilled opponent, whittle him or her down to a realistic size in your own mind, then focus on the strengths of your own game. Give yourself permission to play your best.

The Zone: A Flow of Permission

When you're in the Zone, or a state of Go, you allow your Multiple Imagery System to process information. It's not a forced effort in your conscious mind but an automatic process in your subconscious. When in a state of Go, no matter their level, players display the following characteristics:

1. Verbally quiet, especially over the ball, with no internal arguments.

2. Decisive and committed to the shot.

3. Relaxed, except for selective tension. Tension and anxiety shut down imagery, therefore an overall sense of muscle relaxation allows your multiple imagery system to function on high.

4. Absence of manipulation. They are carried along by the 30-Second Swing and the momentum of the round.

5. No prejudging of the shot's consequences, no notion of bad before it happens. The game just is. When you're in the Zone, you get rid of the baggage of consequences.

In the Hawaiian Open in 1994, Davis Love was on track to break 59. He said, "When I was putting for eagle on the 13th, I was thinking, 'If I make this, I have a shot at 59.' That's the only time I lost focus." Love missed that 15-foot eagle putt, and found his momentum broken. He hit a poor iron on the next hole and then missed a makeable birdie putt on the 15th. But, like a great champion, he regained his focus, and reestablished his momentum and went on to shoot 60, a course record.

When you start thinking about future consequences, treat it as a warning signal that reminds you to get your mind back on golf.

Recognizing Go Signals

It's easy to identify a Go signal, the end result of the permission sequence. When you're over the ball your mind is quiet. This doesn't mean it's silent, but there isn't any high-pitched chatter. Your internal voice is calm and supportive. You're committed to your plan, and resolute about the shot you've chosen to play. You're excited, but it's the anticipation of something good, not the fear of something bad. Under these conditions, your best golf is effortless as you're carried along from shot to shot by a constant flow of Go signals.

Just before he accepted the trophy for winning the 2000 U.S. Open, where he decimated the field by 15 shots, Tiger Woods described perfect permission in a state of Go. "All week I've had a sense of calmness that I haven't had in a while, reminiscent of how I played at Augusta in '97. I felt very tranquil, very calm, even in the midst of the stormy conditions yesterday, I still felt very peaceful inside. For some reason no matter what happened out there I was able to keep my cool and my composure and focus 100 percent on each and every shot."

But what happens when your brain sends you a No signal, a warning that something is wrong with your plan? Is there a way to turn No signals into Go signals?

FALL IN LOVE WITH YOUR GO'S BUT LISTEN
TO YOUR NO'S

It's easy to dislike No signals and to treat them as an unwanted by-product of playing golf, but nothing could be further from the truth. No signals are the emotional counterpart of a body-wide warning network that keeps you safe. This network includes the pain system, which tells you when your body is being damaged; the balance system, which warns you when you're about to fall down, and the hunger/thirst system, which alerts you when supplies are running low.

Signals like pain and hunger may be uncomfortable but, if they weren't, we wouldn't pay attention to them. In the same way, No signals, by their nature, must produce some measure of discomfort, a volume of perturbations sufficient to spur action. It is no wonder that the more outlandish and fanciful your shot plans are, the stronger the amplitude of the message: NO MEANS NO!

THE NO SIGNAL AT AUGUSTA

Fred Couples described playing through a No signal on the 13th hole at Augusta National when he was leading the 1998 Masters, which cost him the championship. "My thought process on the tee was I hit three perfect drives there and [there was] a little bit of wind . . . we're talking just enough to play with you. I tried to hit it a little harder and overcooked it and it hit a branch and went way left, and I ended up hitting a sand wedge. You know, anything could have happened, but I got it through the trees back down on the fairway. Then I had 162 to the flag and may have panicked a little bit. It was a seven-iron shot, and we talked about just hitting six and getting out of there. It's very hard

to do that when you know you have too much club. I tried to
hit it higher and easier and it just went in the creek." Even a
great champion like Couples must pay the price for ignoring
a No signal.

DR. NO AND THE BATTLE FOR YOUR BRAIN

Architects, by their course design, create No signals, messages of
doubt and confusion that are like silent torpedoes sent to sink
the ships of the unsuspecting golfers. As Robert Trent Jones Jr.
has described, it's a trick of designers to position a tee so the
wind will divert the attention of the player and cause uncer-
tainty. This is one reason so many golfers hit the ball well on the
practice range but not as well on the golf course—there are no
No signals built into the practice range. Then again, the architect doesn't need to defend the driving range, but he does care
about defending his golf course. When he was asked if the latest
high-tech golf equipment was a threat to his golf courses, Jones
Jr. replied, "Do you think that the armament-builders in
medieval times were worried when gunpowder came in and
bows and arrows went out? Of course, I worry! I have to figure
out some new defenses." And the word defenses was not idly
chosen.

One of golf's most exciting aspects is the fact that the architect is trying to run your brain and you're trying to prevent it. If
golf were a movie it might be titled *Invasion of the Brain Snatchers.*
One of the chief brain snatchers, Pete Dye, was honest enough
when he said, "When you get those dudes thinking, they're in
trouble." And not only do they want you thinking about what
evil lurks on the courses, they want you to be visually intimi-
dated when you see the monsters. They present you with a
threatening array of bunkers, mounds, water, humpback greens,
and railway ties—and these are just the obvious intimidators.

Euphemistically called challenges, architects arrange them to strike fear into the golfer's heart. As Jones Jr. said, "Some tees are positioned with some psychological elements in mind. For example, some tees are positioned to . . . create a certain intimidation factor for the golfer. . . . Designers love to use this technique to create indecisiveness about your club and shot selection."

Once the human brain realizes it is being consistently fooled and penalized for failure, it assumes it's under attack. The brain responds by mobilizing the fight/flight response, a producer of antigolf chemicals that flood your body and make it impossible to play your best golf. Architects try to introduce a series of No signals designed to create mental havoc with all its associated emotions. If you're not in control of your modes, this mental havoc reverberates through your 30-Second Swing. You hit bad shots, berate yourself, and blame your swing, then rush to the driving range to change it. This endless cycle can go on for years; though the particulars are interchangeable, the pattern is the same.

"Gee, It Doesn't Look That Far"

Although it may be sitting right in front of you, architects make it difficult to locate the target accurately because they create optical illusions designed to fool you. Legendary architect Alister Mackenzie was a camouflage expert during World War I, so he knew a good bit about fooling the eye. His colleagues, past and present, are all practitioners of the same art. Using disguise and deception, a skilled golf course architect can hide a target in plain sight.

Donald Ross was famous for his use of bunkers, building them 20 or so yards from the green. By raising the front lip, he made them appear as though they were greenside bunkers. You may know the exact yardage to the pin but illusions, such as Ross's bunkers, make the distance look different. The groundwork for confusion is set.

Architects use mounds and trees in the same way. A green surrounded by tall trees always looks closer than it really is because the brain assumes large objects are nearby. How many times have you looked at the moon and thought that you could almost reach out and touch it? The opposite is true of small objects, which the brain assumes are farther away. Knowing this, architects strategically place mounds to make pins look short or greens seem smaller than they are, making the greens appear farther than the yardage indicates. This is one reason why you never get tired of playing brilliantly designed courses. With the golf ball in a different place each time you play, the scope of the optical illusion changes, and that keeps your brain on its toes and the challenge new and exciting.

If you're not running your brain well as you progress from illusion to illusion, shot to shot, hole to hole, your brain shuttles between twinges of hesitation and cascades of confusion. Golf is the ultimate mind game and it can make your head spin. Architects love to play with your brain so they can run your game, but you don't have to let them.

It is this wonderful battle for your mental screen, with your brain as the battleground that's the fascinating feature of the game. Sometimes it's not really about winning or recognition or even about score. That's just how you keep track of who's in control—if it's a low score, you were in control; if it's a high score, the architect was in control. Architects try to run your mental screen by making the trouble loom large, while you're trying to run your own brain by putting the target on your screen. This battle is the essence of the game and, if you don't realize this unique challenge of golf, then it is indeed a good walk spoiled.

TURNING NO INTO GO

The course design is not the only element that can cause No signals. They come from a variety of sources. It could be a message that you've chosen the wrong plan, or you don't have enough information to execute the plan. It could be that you're stressed out or feeling jumpy. No signals come in bunches when the wind is blowing or you have to work your way around hazards like bunkers and water when your A and B game have deserted you. Thus, all golfers receive No signals, for they are inherent to the game. The difference is that better planners receive fewer No signals, and when they do receive them, they know how to convert them to Go signals. The specific difference between a good player and a great player, at every talent level, is how each deals with their No signals. At the championship level, ignoring even one No signal can be disastrous, just as it can be for you in the club championship, a two-dollar bet with your pals, or a nine-hole round by yourself after work.

Knowing how important these golf messages are is only one step in running your brain. Next you must learn how to change a No to a Go and finally you must become an expert at the actual conversion.

SCIENCE SUPPORTS NO/GO SIGNALS

While his research was not designed to document the existence of No and Go signals, Dr. Richard Lonetto did just that when he recorded golfers' heart rates to determine how they perform under stress. The subjects were fifteen Tour players, and fifteen amateurs with handicaps ranging from 2 to 23. He found two different heartbeat patterns: one associated with good shots and one associated with bad shots.

The Good Shot Pattern
A wavelike pattern emerged for good shot making, consisting of three phases.

Phase 1: In the preparation phase heart rates averaged 10–30 percent above individual baselines. During this phase the golfer

SHOT HEART RATE

Good Shot Heart Rate Pattern

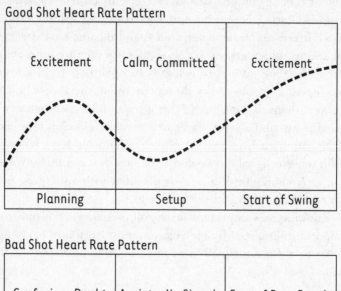

Excitement	Calm, Committed	Excitement
Planning	Setup	Start of Swing

Bad Shot Heart Rate Pattern

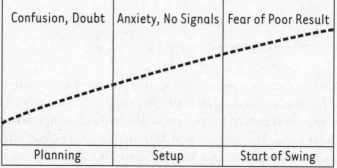

Confusion, Doubt	Anxiety, No Signals	Fear of Poor Result
Planning	Setup	Start of Swing

selected a club, visualized the shot, and was receiving and processing information about the target. At the start of this phase the heart rates were found to be at their highest level, ranging from 100 to 120 beats a minute. They began to slow down, however, as the golfer entered the next phase.

Phase 2: In the commitment phase, as they are over the ball and entering the execution mode, the subject's heart rate continued to decrease, reaching their lowest levels in a range of 65–92 beats per minute.

Phase 3: In the action phase, heart rates rose during the backswing and peaked through the impact zone.

When asked how they felt throughout the process, the golfers reported feeling solid, in balance, and calm. They felt decisive about their plan, and were completely committed to the shot they had chosen to play. There was an excitement, but it was the anticipation of something good. There were "butterflies" but they were flying in formation.

These feelings provided a personal trigger for them, a Go signal, indicating that the moment had come to start the swing. In fact, the golfers described the feeling when their heart rate dropped as being in rhythm, or feeling in sync. This is part of being in the Zone, a condition where the conscious and subconscious mind are in agreement, and full permission is granted.

The Bad Shot Pattern

When these same players hit bad golf shots, there was a distinctly different pattern related to the heart rate. The initial increase in heart rate during the preparation stage was similar, but as they progressed through the phases, their heart rate continued to climb. They described themselves as being anxious, and indecisive, and filled with negative internal chatter. They were unsure of their plan and, as such, they were not totally committed to the shot. Instead of excitement, anticipation, and a ready-to-go feeling, there was uneasiness, a classic description of a No signal. As you've learned, if you continually ignore your No signals, you will never reach your golfing potential, no matter how good your swing is.

COMMON NO SIGNALS

There are many types of No signals and each person has their own set. Below I have outlined a few of the most common that you are likely to encounter as you play. I advise you to keep track of them and structure your practice sessions around them. The better you are at handling your No signals, the better your golf game will be.

THE DOUBT NO SIGNAL

Your subconscious won't let you try a shot you shouldn't without broadcasting a Doubt No signal. This No signal is a distinct feeling that you've chosen the wrong shot plan. Your brain is saying, "No, you don't have this shot." Since your subconscious doesn't like your shot selection, it won't send a Go signal, so there's no sense in arguing. Just step away from the ball and rethink the shot.

Doubt signals simply indicate that you're not ready to play. You've lost your final commitment and must reestablish it by presenting your subconscious with a better plan. While you want to clear up any doubts before you pull the trigger, Doubt No signals can be put to good use because they tell you where your weaknesses lie.

GO DAYS AND NO DAYS

Following are several examples of Doubt signals and the repercussions of how you handle them. Remember that all golfers receive No signals but champions know how to change them into Go signals.

SITUATION 1

Instead of playing safely to the layup area, you decide to attempt a long carry over water to a pin cut behind the hazard. As you address the ball, you have a strong feeling that you're going to hit it into the water. Your brain is sending you a message that translates, "Warning, you don't have the correct plan for this shot." What do you do?

On a Bad Brain Running Day

Your conscious mind intervenes and tells you that you can create the shot by changing your swing. So you ignore your subconscious and, to compensate for the No signal, you exaggerate your finish to keep the ball in the air a little longer. You've switched games without even realizing it. You're now playing Golf Swing, a game where the goal is to put your swing mechanics in perfect order. That's different from golf, a game where the goal is to get the ball to the target. Predictably, by trying to manipulate your swing, you come out of the shot through impact, catch it just a tad thin, and knife it into the hazard. Then you get mad and, by emotionalizing the event, you create a heavy Track of Failure in your brain. (More on this in Chapter 9.)

On a Good Brain Running Day

Your response is to acknowledge the No signal, step away from the ball, and *change your plan*—you aim for the bail-out area instead of the flag. When you do, your brain will signal you that you've made the right choice and you can send the ball to the target in a state of Go.

SITUATION 2

It's cart path only and your ball is in the middle of the fairway. The pin is directly behind a bunker and you're taking dead aim at the flag with a nine-iron. It crosses your mind that although you're a good bunker player, if you mishit this shot a bit with this high-lofted iron, it could plug in the bunker. Your brain has sent you a No signal that you need a new plan. What do you do?

On a Bad Brain Running Day

Since your cart and clubs are back on the path, you tell yourself that it will take too long to walk back and switch clubs; after all, it's 20 yards away and you don't want to hold up play. Besides, walking back to the cart would show everyone that you had made a mistake. By ignoring your No signal, you've switched games. A few seconds ago, you were playing golf, and suddenly you're playing What Will People Think of Me?, a game where you change your behavior so people won't think ill of you.

Driven by a strong suspicion that you're using the wrong club, you overswing in an attempt to hit the ball harder. You make off-center contact and the ball drops straight down and buries in the sand against the lip. The nasty lie neutralizes your bunker skill and you make bogey. You mutter, "That's just my luck," which, of course, it is when you're not running your brain very well.

On a Good Brain Running Day

On a good brain running day, you always bring at least three clubs when it's "cart path only." After you receive the No signal, you go through your 30-Second Swing again, redoing your plan until your subconscious likes your shot selection. You switch to your eight-iron, which will get you to the center of the green, though it's a half-club too much to put you close to the pin. In a state of Go, you strike the ball solidly, a gust of wind balloons the ball just enough to drop it next to the pin. You congratulate yourself on your great planning and roll in an easy birdie.

Please remember that the better you plan, the luckier you'll be and, overall, the faster you'll play. It takes less time to make a well-planned birdie than it does to rush into a bogey.

SITUATION 3

With out of bounds on the right, you've aimed your driver down the center of the fairway. Your normal shot shape is right to left but, and as you address the ball, you feel a gust of wind over your left shoulder and receive a Doubt No signal. Your brain is telling you you're going to slice the ball out of bounds. What do you do?

On a Bad Brain Running Day

You love hitting your driver and you're usually the longest hitter in your group. Your opponent already bombed one, and you feel the need to answer. Ignoring the No signal, your plan involves simply hitting this tee shot as hard as you can. Without realizing it, you've switched games. You're now playing Long-Drive Champion, a game where superior distance is the goal but, like most long drive champions, you hit it long and wrong. Trying to kill it, you rotate your upper body too quickly, leaving the club face open at impact, causing a big slice—OB.

On a Good Brain Running Day

You ignore your opponent's distance challenge, pay attention to golf, and honor your No signal. You drop down to a two-iron and, although it's a par-5 hole you can sometimes reach in two, you lay up to avoid the slice out of bounds. You make an easy par while Mr. Long Ball goes for the green in two, fails, and ends up making a seven. He wins at Spectacular Golf but you win at Scoring Golf.

THE CONFUSION NO SIGNAL

Overall, your plan may be okay, but you can't generate a Go signal when your plan is based on insufficient information. If you don't give it the data it needs, your brain sends you a confusion No signal. Simply put, your brain won't let you fire at a target when it doesn't know where the target is.

Confusion No signals often occur in windy conditions. For example, you've chosen a seven-iron, the perfect club to carry the bunker and land the ball near the hole. You go through the early stages of your 30-Second Swing, address the ball, and take your final look at the target. As you do, you feel a gust of wind on your cheek. Do you still have the correct club in your hand? Should you swing a little harder than you had planned, or should you change clubs? You're confused because your brain knows you haven't taken into consideration the gusting winds. In effect, you don't know where the target is. The only route to a Go signal is to back off and gather the information you're missing.

It Can Make Your Head Spin

A major cause of Confusion No signals is the architect's use of optical illusions that are specifically designed to make you think the target is somewhere that it isn't. Cavemen didn't have yardage books, but nevertheless they became experts at judging how far away an object was by eyeing it. A species can form a strong habit doing something for a million years, so when the yardage marker reads 150 yards, but your eyes say 130 yards (thanks to the architect's optical illusion), what information do you act on? What you see or what the yardage marker indicates? This generates a Confusion No signal, a powerful defense in the hands of an architect.

CONTROLLING THE LOOM CAN CONTROL NO SIGNALS

A major-league strategy for running your brain involves controlling your mental screen where images of your world are represented—close your eyes and you can see yours. When you play golf, your golfing experience is displayed on your screen, the bunkers, out of bounds, water hazards, the size of the greens, the width of the driving areas, etc. They are represented in your mind, as you *subjectively* evaluate them, not necessarily as they really are. So if you're driving the ball wildly, the 50-yard-wide fairway looks like a bowling lane. If you're driving it straight, the same fairway looks like you could land a 747 in it. Since it's *your interpretation* that fills your mental screen, you can fill it with hazards, or targets—it's your choice. Fill your screen with the hazards and you'll receive No signals; fill it with the target and you've laid the groundwork to receive a Go signal.

Here's an example of how it works. You have an approach shot over a water hazard to a pin in front of the green and you're worried about making a par. It appears, in your mind, that the landing area is minuscule, while the hazard looms large on your mental screen. In reality, the lake is large, but you only have to carry a short span of water and there is plenty of room for the ball (it's only about 1.68 inches around) in the middle of the green. The way you evaluate the situation makes the hazard appear large on your screen, relative to a tiny green. This representation, BIG HAZARD/small target, convinces your brain that the situation is hopeless, and this is relayed in the form of a No signal.

The key is that if your perception causes the trouble to loom large, then you also have the power to make the trouble recede to a manageable size. Why not make the flagstick or the fairway loom large for every shot? You can do this by closing your eyes, picturing the scene, and making the trouble shrink on your mental screen. In this way, you can change perceived No signals into Go signals. And with a bit of mental discipline, you can become a master of this skill.

The Woman and the Water

A good example of a shift in perspective is a student of mine who couldn't carry a 30-foot-wide creek fronting a green on a short par-3. It was an 80-yard shot, with 25 yards of fairway between the creek and the green. This distance was ordinarily no problem for her. It wasn't a matter of swing mechanics or distance; she was merely responding to her perception of the situation. The creek, which should have only been part of the background, overwhelmed the other parts of the picture on her mental screen to loom large. To her optical system, it was 30 feet wide, but to her visual system, it was 300 feet wide and nonnegotiable.

I took her to the other side of the creek and had her stand beside the green and look back toward the tee. From this perspective, she could see what a large landing area there was between the creek and the green, and how narrow the creek actually was. Then I asked her to tee up a ball and hit it back toward the tee, which she did, clearing the water with no problem at all.

Due to a change in perspective, the images on her mental screen changed. She shrank the trouble and moved it from the foreground to background where it belonged, and she never had the problem again. By changing her perspective, she regained control of her mental screen. She learned to run her own brain, rather than allowing the situation to run it for her.

> **A GOOD WALK BACKWARD**
> Tour caddies and players often walk a course backward before a tournament to gain a different perspective on the course. If you're having trouble with a particular hole, look back at the spot where you played from and then the landing area you had available to you. You'll usually find there's more room than you saw when standing over the ball. With a more informed perspective on your next visit, you can better plan and execute the shot that fits the reality of the situation.

A GEOMETRY NO SIGNAL: BALL POSITION

Whatever else this game is, it's a game of geometry—spatial relationships composed of patterns of lines and angles that link the player to the target. Whether you like geometry or not, your brain loves it, and deals with it on a regular basis. The brain breaks down all your experience into geometric shapes for storage. When you need to recall something, such as a person's face or the shape of the Empire State Building, your brain reassembles the geometric shapes it has stored. Since the most basic relationship in golf is your relationship to the ball, or ball position, if it goes awry, a Geometry No signal results. When you get the feeling that something just doesn't look right as you gaze down at the ball, your subconscious is telling you to adjust your ball position.

DISTRESS NO SIGNAL

Some situations are more stressful than others and it is a matter of individual perception that causes the golfer to cross the line from good stress that pumps you up to distress that tears you down. Distress gives off its own warning signal, a tension No signal that you must be sure to heed.

The best way to beat Distress No signals is to spot check the tension in your muscles. Start at the top and let your jaw and face muscles go limp. Then relax your neck and shoulder muscles, using a soft shrugging action. Last, you should have an oily feeling in your wrists, with your arms hanging relaxed at address like those of a gorilla. Your grip pressure, on a range of 1 to 10, should be about a 6. Combine these distress busters with a deep abdominal breath, and you can relax into a flow to Go.

SOMEWHERE BETWEEN TIN MAN AND SCARECROW

But it is important to note that your goal is not to be totally relaxed at any point during your 30-Second Swing. At address, for example, you should feel somewhere in the middle between trip-wire-tense and limp, a feeling I call selective tension, where some of your muscles are tense and ready for action and others are relaxed (see above). At address you should feel some tension in your lower back area, and the insides of your thighs, ankles, and the inner rim of each foot. You should also feel a light adhesion between your arms and your upper chest. Remember the acronym STTOP: Selective Tension Turns On Power, a phrase that will remind you to scan your body looking for unwanted tightness.

There are other ways to combat distress. As you'll learn later in this book, holding your breath increases the overall tension level in your body, so in between shots, breathe deep in your stomach and expel the air to a rhythmic count. If you have eye-strain, open your eyes wide and close them three or four times to produce some lubrication. Stare far away for fifteen seconds, then close your eyes and gently massage your eyes with the palms of your hands.

TIME IQ

Sometimes your swing is completely under your control. It's smooth and syrupy and you feel powerful in an unhurried sort of way. Other times your swing is a like a Chinese fire drill, with helter-skelter, jerky movements more Mel Brooks than Mark Brooks. Instead of making a golf swing, you throw a fit. It is important to realize that fluctuations in your Time IQ are a common cause of No signals. But why is that? How can your Time IQ fluctuate so wildly?

In part, the psychological stress of situations like 1st tee jitters or a problem in your business or love life fouls your Time IQ. But it's also the natural and ongoing changes of your bodily systems. You are a bundle of intertwined cycles, intellectual, physical, and emotional. Circadian rhythms hold sway over you and there are times when you're tired, sick, newly in love, or recently divorced. For this reason, you're not exactly the same person from week to week, month to month, round to round, or even sometimes from hole to hole. Yet when you change you don't lose your memory of how to swing the club in three dimensions—what you lose is your sense of time.

Since Time IQ disruptions manifest themselves as mechanical swing flaws, the danger is that you will try to treat the effect rather than the cause. Make it a rule that you never make a change in your swing to rectify a timing problem. If you violate that rule you'll fall victim to that all too common affliction: Sudden and Inexplicable Golf Swing Disappearance Syndrome. When you start to produce errant shots, always troubleshoot your Time IQ before you do anything else.

TIME IQ NO SIGNAL

When you feel pressed for time, your brain is sending you a No signal. To bring your Time IQ (how you handle the dimension of time) back under your control, you need to move in what may seem like slow motion. When you catch yourself rushing, image yourself at half speed. Drive your cart slowly, walk and talk slowly, slow down your eye movements (don't let them dart around), stop at the water cooler even if you're not thirsty, and arrive last on the tee box. In other words, do everything you can to counter your tendency to speed up under pressure.

Check for symptoms of timing problems with the following questions. Are you jumping at the ball? Forcing the club to the ball? Suddenly hitting uncharacteristic shots and taking deep divots? Are you hitting off-center shots with no pattern—some off the toe and some off the heel of your club? Are you driving the golf cart faster and recklessly? Are you walking and talking faster than normal, with more internal conversation?

A small number of golfers lose control of their Time IQ by slowing down instead of speeding up. They appear listless and walk as if they're on a death march. Their speech is slow and their faces expressionless. These golfers need to speed up when their Time IQ is off.

Beating the Time IQ No Signal

When your Time IQ deteriorates on the course the first area it affects is the transition from your backswing to your downswing. Make sure that you slow your swing enough to give the club time to change direction. During the transition at the top, your club head not only reverses direction and starts back toward the target but, if you give it enough time, it will also drop down before it starts targetward. This slight deepening of the club head just as you start down puts it in perfect position to approach the ball from inside the target line, the most powerful and accurate striking angle.

Scotty, the cantankerous engine room genius in *Star Trek*, knew about time. Captain Kirk would get in a jam and order Scotty to apply full power. Invariably, Scotty would plead, "I need more time, Captain, I need more time!" Like Scotty, when you're under pressure, you need more time at the top of your swing.

There Is No Now in the Golf Swing

The other danger point with regard to time is the impact zone. The hit impulse is the ever-present inclination to apply additional force to the golf ball. When it is mistimed, both the club face position and the path of your club are adversely affected. To counteract the hit impulse, there shouldn't be a NOW in your swing. There's no point where you can identify the feeling of hitting as in, "Not now, not now, here it comes, it's almost here, NOW!"

To recalibrate your Time IQ and change the No to Go, start by changing your image of what happens from the top of your swing. On your mental screen, picture the start of your downswing like a plane taxiing down a runway, gaining speed and power gradually rather than bursting away like a dragster.

WWPTOM NO SIGNAL

Switching games can generate serious No signals. Keep in mind that different games have different rules and different outcomes and each game should be played so that the rules and the outcomes match up. If you're playing WWPTOM (What Will People Think of Me?), a common game that brains like to play, then play by the rules, which are:

1. Consider a certain behavior.
2. Shape that behavior so that the people who observe it will think well of you.
3. If this is unsuccessful, you need to find a new behavior and/or new people to shape it to. The outcome of this game is deemed a success if you think the people watching you like what you do.

For example, you're a fast player who doesn't want to hold up the other members of your group. You play even faster when there's a group coming up behind you. Your goal is not to annoy the group behind you by making them wait, so you hurry your shots. Finally, when rushing causes you to hit a clunker, you pick the ball up and don't even finish the hole. You haven't recorded a score, but that's okay because you're not playing golf, you're playing WWPTOM, and that doesn't involve a golf score. Just don't get mad at yourself on the next tee for a lousy golf performance— you played WWPTOM perfectly.

Keep Your Games Straight

In golf, your concern is the target and getting the ball into the hole in order to record the lowest score you can on each hole. Note that there is nothing in the definition of golf that mentions people behind you and what they are thinking about you. Now you may be receiving No signals, but you need to make sure they're game-of-golf No signals, not WWPTOM No signals.

Thus, an essential aspect of running your own brain is to keep your games separate, and know what game you're playing at all times. Don't play WWPTOM and then use your golf score to rate how successful you are—you're mismatching the rules of one game with the outcomes of another, and this can only destroy your confidence.

And this game is not limited to the amateur ranks; WWPTOM is played regularly on the pro tours too.

"My dear, I don't give a damn."

In his early years on the PGA Tour, Mark O'Meara had his struggles, despite earning Rookie of the Year honors. In a tournament at Pinehurst, he played in a group with Hale Irwin. Irwin shot lights-out while O'Meara hit it all over the lot and finished with a 78. As they walked off the 18th green, an embarrassed O'Meara apologized to Irwin for his poor play. Irwin, one of golf's champion brain runners, put his arm around the young player and said, "Nothing personal, Mark, but frankly, I don't give a damn how you played." Irwin was playing golf, O'Meara was playing WWPTOM, and both were experts at their games that day.

Tour player Paul Goydos once said, "All of a sudden, it isn't just about the golf; you start hitting bad shots and you begin to worry about what your playing partner thinks of you, or your game, or worse, what the gallery is thinking. Everything becomes so big in your mind you realize later that the only person to whom it was that big was you." Learning this is a major part of becoming a champion. When you turn inside yourself and get a case of the "I's" your ego tells you that everybody's looking at you and cares what you're doing. Actually, they're all worried about themselves.

NO SIGNAL TRACKER

When you first use it, keep your No signal tracker every round for at least five rounds. Then you can back off if you like to one out of every ten rounds. Whatever the frequency, your goal is to find out under what circumstances you're denied full permission. Identify the situations that cause bad outcomes. For instance, a left-to-right wind causes you to slice the ball; a distracting member of your group or the dawdling of the group ahead of you ruins your shot. Bad outcomes in these kinds of situations are just as much weaknesses in your Strength and Weakness Profile as poor bunker play or errant drives. The goal is that over time you will progressively eliminate all the recurring situations in which you receive No signals.

THE NO TO GO SUMMARY

To play golf like a champion at any talent level, you must be able to run your own brain rather than letting the situations you encounter on the golf course run it for you. To do so, you have to: (1) be able to recognize No signals and Go signals, (2) know how to convert No to Go, and (3) actually make this conversion.

Step 3 is the stumbling block for most people. If you know the techniques, but fail to implement them, your knowledge will have no power at all. In working with my students, I have found the following exchange all too common: "Did you get a No signal on that shot?" Answer: "Yes I did." "What did you do about it?" Answer: "Nothing; I went ahead and swung anyway."

As you incorporate each technique into your 30-Second Swing, you add more resources to your arsenal, and you'll receive more and more Go signals. At first, you may have to step away from the ball a number of times each round. Remember, you are in a learning situation and it will take time

No Signal Tracking Chart

For each No signal you receive, check the box that best describes its cause. If you receive a Go signal, check the Go! box. After the round, match a solution to each No signal. Also, total each column so you have an idea of which No signal you are most susceptible to. Add the information to your Strength and Weakness Profile and work on the solutions.

Doubt	Confusion	WWPTOM	Rushing	Tension	External	Swing Feel	?	Go!	Solution#
		✓							2
								✓	
						✓			5
			✓						2
								✓	
								✓	
								✓	
	✓								1
Total	Total	Total	Total	Total	Total	Total	Total	Total	

Solutions

1 = Replan / Reimage   2 = Modify internal voice   3 = Control loom (mental screen)
4 = Relax   5 = Rehearsal swing   6 = Time IQ

NOTE: WWPTOM = What Will People Think of Me?
External = Distractions such as unexpected noises, wind shift, beverage cart, etc.

but, with patience, perseverance, and practice, you'll master the art of listening to your signal system and then applying the appropriate techniques. When you do, you'll play up to your talent level for each and every shot—and that is all you can ask of yourself.

CHAPTER 6

The Power of Imagery

> I am enough of an artist to draw freely upon my imagination. Imagination is more important than knowledge. Knowledge is limited. Imagination encircles the world.
>
> —ALBERT EINSTEIN

INTRODUCTION

NOW THAT YOUR PLAN for the shot is clear, at this point in your 30-Second Swing you'll magnify and strengthen it by using the Power of Imagery. After making a plan, most golfers revert to thoughts of swing mechanics and catastrophic scenarios before they even address the ball. This debilitating habit wastes the Power of Imagery and robs them of their golf potential.

Instead of swing mechanics and negative thoughts, you need to occupy your mind with success images centered on the target. You have to create images that are so real to your brain it responds by automatically cueing your muscles to get the job done. As Dr. Emile Coué outlined in his book *Self-Mastery Through Conscious Autosuggestion,* there are two basic principles involved in imaging: (1) Your mental screen can image only one thing at a time and, (2) when we concentrate on a thought, the thought becomes true because our body transforms it into action.

Thus, images direct motor responses. Your brain makes a collage of images then synthesizes these images into a fine-tuned experience. For each shot you feel the wind, hear it blowing, see the flag flutter, and your brain automatically calculates its effect on your shot. Your brain then translates the information into movements designed to satisfy the plan that you have made. On cue, your arms swing and your body turns, all at a speed and a pace that will send the ball to target. You can understand now why you need to become a master at imaging—imagery, well managed, is powerful stuff.

THE POWER OF IMAGERY

Much of the brain's energy is devoted to producing imagery, and since your brain only allocates its resources to important matters, imagery must be a high-powered tool in human performance—a power you must harness to run your brain.

Your brain gathers its images through each of your five senses. You see an object, smell it, touch it, taste it, and/or hear it. The object emits information about itself that you filter through your senses and then store in your memory. In this way, you learn about your world—and the more you experience and record, the more accurately you can recall your world in detail whenever you need to. In addition, since images cue motor responses, the ability to re-create images on your mental screen is a valuable ally in your repertoire of resources.

Multisensorial Imaging

An important part of your 30-Second Swing is a multisensorial image of the shot you are about to play—call it an instant pre-play. The most powerful images, those that can motivate you to action, are multisensorial. You see the shot in great detail, framed against the blue sky; you see the ball curve, its trajectory and its final resting place next to the pin or in the middle of the fairway. You hear the solid splat of a dead-center contact and feel the balance of a perfect swing, the rhythm of a well-struck shot.

Associated vs. Dissociated

The ability to change from an associated state to a dissociated state is a power you should cultivate. A dissociated state is one of objectivity and dispassion in which you are involved in a particular event as an observer and evaluator. You're not involved as a protagonist. You care but there are no major-league emotions that affect your performance. On the other hand, in the associated state, the emotional mode reigns and you are intimately linked to the event.

You can switch states whenever it's helpful, if you want to. Doctors treating patients with horrific injuries in emergency rooms learn to dissociate long enough to concentrate solely on providing lifesaving treatment. Medics who routinely faced severe life-threatening conditions were comparatively stress-free in the field. In order to do their job they had learned to dissociate.

When two people are arguing, they are both in an associated state. While it may not solve the disagreement, if one participant switches to a dissociated state, the argument will end. If you find yourself losing it on the golf course, you can learn through practice to switch states, disengage, and prevent yourself from laying down heavyweight Tracks of Failure.

ASSOCIATED IMAGING

Most shot imaging takes place in a dissociated state. You feel and hear the shot whistle away, and see the ball land next to the pin— you're involved because it's your image but, emotionally, there is no personal relationship, you're just a spectator. Though dissociated imaging is better than not imaging at all, you'll more fully tap your Power of Imagery if you become emotionally involved.

To maximize your imaging power, learn to personalize your images; instead of simply having an image, you become the image. It's not just you looking at you on the screen. When you have an associated image, the image is the reality. You're experiencing the feelings of what's happening to you, just as you do when the experience is real and you are fully absorbed in it.

You can become so good at associated imaging that your central nervous system won't be able to tell the difference between a real experience and a perfectly imagined one. This means that your shot plan has the huge advantage of a test drive before you swing. Primed by these virtual images of the way things should be, the shot itself is almost anticlimactic.

While imaging every shot may sound like a long and involved process, the power of which is available to only a few, this is not the case. Every golfer has the Power of Imagery available to them if they would just practice it.

Brain scans may shed light on how people can improve their golf games by simply imagining they are hitting a golf shot. Dr. Richard Frackowiak, professor of cognitive neurology at the Institute of Neurology in London, gives a scientific explanation for the experiences of performers like pianists, violinists, and golfers, who normally rehearse their skill mentally before executing it physically.

In his study, brain scans were taken of six men as they

moved a joystick in a certain pattern. The scans were repeated as the men simply imagined moving the joystick. The scans showed that the imagined experience used 80 percent of the brain circuitry used in the actual physical experience. Frackowiak says, "All the brain areas dealing with the movement activate, except for the region associated with the final command that says, 'Go.' "

Thus when you image a golf swing correctly the mental image turns on a large percentage of the neural networks used when you swing for real, and that strengthens the brain cell connections needed to make a good swing. Imaging is the ultimate tool in creating Tracks of Excellence, as you'll learn in Chapter 9.

THE ASSOCIATED IMAGING TECHNIQUE

Step One—Choose a Model

Select the model for the skill you want to learn. Let's say you want to improve your short-iron play, so you choose the model of Tiger Woods hitting a short-iron.

Step Two—Study the Model

You study the model (a tape of his swing) as a dissociated observer until every time you call up the image, it's perfect. In this example, you watch the tape until you can see your Tiger image clearly and distinctly. The image is flawless—Tiger in his red shirt making the swing . . . the ball in the air . . . then landing 10 feet beyond the flag . . . spinning back, and then, as if it were on a string, it disappears into the hole.

Step 3—Alter the Model

Next, call up your image but this time see yourself as the model. Though you're still dissociated, now you're watching yourself hit that shot. Practice this step so that every time you recall that scene, you are the star of the image.

Step 4—You Become the Model

Finally, you become the model by associating with it. You feel the thrill of holing a short-iron from the fairway. Due to the rush of chemicals this excitement produces, your brain thinks you've actually holed the shot.

THERE MUST BE SOMETHING TO IT, IF THEY ALL DO IT

There must be something to this "imagery stuff" if so many great champions use it. When he arrived at the 1965 U.S. Open at Bellerive Country Club, Gary Player said that he was walking past the leader board before the tournament started and he imagined he saw his name at the top as the winner. It seemed so real to him that he felt his victory was a *fait accompli*. Four days later, at the completion of the tournament, he saw his name there for real.

Johnny Miller, once the best player in the world, use to practice by sitting in a chair, closing his eyes, and picturing his swing motion not just once but swing after swing.

Jack Nicklaus, a notoriously slow player in his most successful years, was asked what he was thinking about as he stood over a putt. He said that he saw the line of the putt, the ball rolling down that line, the ball going into the hole, then coming back out of the hole, rolling back down the line, and stopping in front of his putter where it had begun—and he wouldn't putt until he'd seen that mental movie. This is how he used his power of imagery to generate a Go signal and he was not about to fire off a shot without it.

Nicklaus describes the process by which he hits a full shot in his book *Golf My Way*.

I never hit a shot, even in practice, without having a very sharp, in-focus picture of it in my head. It's like a color movie. First I "see" where I want it to finish nice and white and sitting up on the bright green grass. Then the scene quickly changes and I see the ball going there; its path, trajectory and shape, even its behavior on landing. Then there's a sort of a fade-out, and the next scene shows me making the kind of swing that will turn the previous images into reality. Only at the end of this short, private Hollywood spectacular do I select the club and step to the ball.

The great Ben Hogan used to play the entire tournament in his mind before it started. Champions like Hogan, Woods, and Nicklaus can make the game come alive in their minds—before, during, and after they are finished playing.

Champions in other professions use imagery as a major success strategy. An experiment was done to determine the extent to which mental imaging was involved when architects design a building. An experienced architect was blindfolded during the act of design. The results showed that he was able to use mental imaging as a major resource in the design process—he built the building perfectly in his mind before a single stone was laid.

Chess masters routinely use imagery to visualize the position of the pieces they would like to have eight to ten moves in advance.

A remarkable example of employing the Power of Imagery comes from Charlie Wilson, one of the world's finest neurosurgeons. Wilson is an expert in a very difficult procedure called a transsphenoidal resection, the removal of a cancer from the pituitary gland. Malcolm Gladwell describes Wilson's reliance on imagery in an article in *The New Yorker* entitled "The Physical Genius": "Charlie Wilson talks about going running every morning and reviewing each of the day's operations in his head—visualizing the entire procedure and each potential outcome in advance. 'It was a virtual rehearsal,' Wilson says, 'so when I was doing the operation, it was as if I was doing it for the second time.' "

One of my students, a talented surgeon herself, came to see me because she was having an awful time learning her golf swing. Though she is athletic, and easily understood the technical concepts, she couldn't quite get the hang of it. During one of our discussions, I asked her how she prepared for surgery. She described a procedure similar to Charlie Wilson's, where she imaged the entire operation, step by step, just before she fell asleep and again as she lay in bed in the morning just after she awoke.

The good doctor's routine is quite common among creative people who use these two transition periods—entering and coming out of sleep—to problem-solve. During these periods, the brain is in an alpha-theta state where brain waves signal a synchronization of the right and left hemispheres of the brain. This state is most conducive to producing multisensorial images so powerful that they can dramatically improve performance.

I suggested to my student that she use her imaging skills to improve her golf swing. Two weeks later she called me from her home in Pittsburgh to tell me of a marked improvement in her swing.

It is my firm belief that what makes this game so hard for most people is the way they go about learning it. If golfers tried to learn their business the way they attempt to learn golf, they'd be broke. And, tongue in cheek, I often tell my students that if we tried to learn sex the way we learn golf, there would be no one left on the planet.

NOT EVERYONE IS VISUAL

In the previous examples, these champions of imagery created visual descriptions, but some people have trouble seeing things on their mental screen. Imaging is the general rubric under which come all the senses that motivate us to action. For example, you may not be comfortable trying to visualize the shot if your primary processing system is kinesthetic (feel) or auditory (hearing, rhythm, cadence). In this case, don't force yourself to visualize. Instead, preview the shot with the sense that is most natural for you.

PUTTING YOUR BRAIN ON SCAN

All humans have the power to create combinations of sense-images, and the more you practice it the more creative you'll become. Use the following process to determine your dominant image system.

During a twenty-four-hour period, put your brain on scan to see what it's doing. Are you making pictures (visual), are you hearing sounds/words (auditory), or are you experiencing feelings (kinesthetic)? The essential times are those transition periods from one mind-body state or activity to another. For example, how do you wake up? As you lie there in bed are you making pictures of getting up, taking a shower, and going to work or are you talking to yourself describing what you are about to do? The nice thing about your brain is that it can inspect itself and all you have to do is be the director of introspection.

Also, track how you change activities. For example, you're sitting at your desk and you decide it's time to hop in the car and go to the golf course. What images motivate you to overcome the inertia of one activity so you can begin another? Does the motivation come in feelings, words, or pictures? Remember images cue behavior, so master the skill of monitoring how you motivate yourself and soon you can control the process. This is another important aspect in running your own brain.

You can discover your lead sense by experimenting with each of the three types. Once you have identified it, practice using that sense until it becomes an automatic part of your 30-Second Swing. Afterward, try enhancing it by adding the other sense systems to your imaging process.

If left unattended, your brain makes images to idle away time, much as a person whittles a stick or doodles on a pad of paper. This is why images continually flit through your mind, on their way to nowhere in particular, but your brain is always busy doing something.

IMAGES YOU CAN USE

There is another important element to understanding imaging: creative imaging. Some of your images are composites, unicorn-type fabrications created to satisfy a need, like when you invent something in your mind by combining various elements from your database. In a dream state, German chemist Friedrich August Kekulé von Stradonitz imagined six snakes linked together, each with its tail in the mouth of the next one. The image suggested a six-sided figure that proved to be the structure of the benzene molecule, the discovery of which was of utmost importance in organic chemistry. This kind of creative imaging is a common method of problem solving.

Another type of image is actual recall of real objects or experiences, and the more senses that are attached to the image, the more real the reproduction becomes as it sits on your mental screen. Certain objects or experiences favor one sense or another. A chocolate bar lends itself to taste images. Thoughts of the Brooklyn Bridge conjure visual images, unless you travel over it every day, and then it will have a feel, a sound, and even a distinct smell. Image-wise, your multisensorial reproduction of the bridge is as close as you can get without actually being there. Should you have a phobia about crossing bridges, this image, entwined as it is with your life script, could so paralyze you that you could not bring yourself to cross it.

If they can do this, then images have a power, and it is wise to be careful which ones you allow to occupy your screen. In golf, if you are in the habit of allowing the trouble to loom on your screen, then it is trouble you will get, with a capital T.

When you arrive at the point where you have a vivid, multisensorial instant preplay before each shot, you will have added the full power of imagery to your catalog of golfing resources.

CHAMPIONS DESCRIBE THEIR IMAGES

Bobby Jones: "The one influence most likely to assure the satisfactory progression of the swing is clear visualization in the player's mind of the movement."

According to his own statements, from the minute Sam Snead approached the ball he could see in his mind the shot he wanted to play. Snead describes how he connected his mind's-eye view to the feel of the shot he was imaging, and once he both saw it and felt it he could make the actual swing itself without thinking about the individual movements. For example, when Snead was asked to describe the technique of hitting a fade he said, "I just think fade."

Seve Ballesteros, a great champion and a creative genius on the golf course, depended on imagery to help him hit shots. To induce confidence, Seve clearly visualized a line stretching from the ball to the target at the beginning and end of his set-up routine. Once everything checked out, Seve's entire body responded by swinging the club reflexively in response to the lucid picture of the shot that had played in his mind's eye.

Seve receives his Go signal from visual imagery, but it could be a feel and rhythm thing, as it is for Fred Couples, or an auditory Go, as it is for Lee Trevino.

YOUR MENTAL SCREEN

As you learned in the last chapter, each of us has a mental screen where our perception of the world is represented. Close your eyes and you will see yours—you can call up the Eiffel Tower, a juicy red apple, or the face of your mother or father. It's your screen, you own it, and you can put anything you want on it, if you have a mind to.

When you play golf, the parts of your golfing experience are pictured on this screen: the bunkers, out of bounds, water hazards, the size of the greens, the width of the driving areas, etc. As we have said, they are represented not necessarily as they really are, but as you subjectively perceive them.

When you're hitting your irons well, you hardly notice the trouble, but when your swing escapes you, a water hazard fronting the green can look enormous compared with a pea-sized landing area. Since your impression is that you face a hopeless situation, your brain reacts by calling for a radical lunge to prevent the ball from going into the water. Of course, by trying to prevent it, you actually cause it to happen.

If your golf swing is so mechanically unsound that you have no idea where the ball is going, no amount of imaging will help. In this case, you need to take your Strength and Weakness Profile to the driving range and upgrade your weaknesses until you're ready to play. But if it's your perception that often causes the trouble to loom, rather than a problem with your golf swing, then your perception can also cause the trouble to recede to a manageable size.

Why not use your intellect, your analytical mode, to run the stimuli, instead of letting them run you?

FIGHT/FLIGHT AND THE RELAXATION RESPONSE

When asked how he handled the pressure of playing professional basketball so well, Charles Barkley replied, "Pressure?
What pressure? Pressure is something you put in tires." In sport
as in life, what is a burial ground for one is a stage for another.
Johnny Miller said that he looked at a pressure situation in tournament play, in front of a large crowd, as a chance to strut his
stuff, an opportunity to show off. Why is it that some human
beings can handle the pressure and others cannot? One factor
certainly is perception.

Perception is an essential element in determining how your
body reacts to an event and studies show that you can learn to
treat an event as nonstressful if you know how.

In the 1960s, author Peter Bourne studied men under
extreme stress in the Vietnam War and documented his work in
a book titled *Men, Stress and Vietnam.* Bourne found that Army
Special Forces troops and medics who routinely faced severe
life-threatening conditions were surprisingly stress-free, in both
their behavior and the level of stress hormones measured in
urine samples.

Now if one can learn to control the reaction to real-life dangerous events, you can certainly learn to control your mind and
body during a round of golf. In order to do this you must have
direct supervision over the physical system know as the relaxation response, the equal and opposite of the fight/flight
response.

A Perfect System for Action, Not for Thinking
Once you learn your golf swing, its form is "in there," stored
permanently in your brain, and your goal is to have total access
to it every time you step up to the ball. You also want complete
access to your golf database so you can make the right choices,
something you can't have when your mental screen is frozen. A
sure way to freeze that screen is with the fight/flight response,

and once it's called into action, your ability to think in images is drastically reduced.

Ten thousand years ago in the forest you hear a noise and, in a microsecond, you scan your database and match the stimulus with your memory images. When your brain sends back the message, "It's a lion! Run for your life!" your fight/flight response is triggered and, without further thought, you run for your life. In order to be able to flee (or stay and fight) effectively, your body is flooded with powerful chemicals. Hormones give you the adrenaline boost that makes you fast and powerful. Sugar pours into your bloodstream as you break down muscle glycogen for a burst of energy. Your blood pressure increases to drive more blood to your muscles, and your breathing quickens to maximize your carbon dioxide and oxygen exchange rates. Automatically, there is a flooding of blood into the big, banded muscles of back, chest, and legs, bringing the additional oxygen necessary for either fighting or fleeing.

A muscle in contraction uses six times more blood than an inactive muscle. Since the amount of blood in the body is finite (about six quarts), the muscles have to borrow the extra blood from somewhere and, in part, it's diverted from the brain. When you deprive the brain of blood, you deprive it of oxygen supply—in this example, not enough to cause any physical impairment but enough to interrupt the normal flow of images. But that's okay because once the decision comes down to fight or flee, you're on automatic pilot.

This fight/flight process is an ideal and ingenious coping strategy when your life is threatened. When you're on the golf course for four-plus hours, however, and you have to make accurate plans and multisensorial images for every shot, you should avoid the perception that you're under attack. Otherwise you'll trigger the fight/flight response and freeze your screen—putting an end to clearheaded thinking. Plus, being under attack for four hours is exhausting, another reason it's best to control the fight/flight message. You need to relax or you'll simply be too tired to play your best.

Remember that as soon as your brain decides it's under attack and the survival instinct kicks in, you're not in charge anymore; your brain is now on automatic. So to stay in control you need to develop a prime-time brain-running skill—you need to be able to summon the relaxation response, the system that keeps fight/flight at bay.

The Relaxation Response

The relaxation response, a human response pattern described by cardiologist Herbert Benson, MD, an acclaimed Harvard Medical School researcher, produces the opposite bodily reactions to fight/flight. It allows you to keep your mental screen fluid and ready to image. To apply the relaxation response to golf, I have outlined two types of patterns, one a minirelaxation technique that you can accomplish in seconds and use while you're playing as part of your 30-Second Swing. The second is a major relaxation technique for use in a quiet, off-course place where you won't be disturbed. The process takes about twenty minutes to complete.

In this chapter, the emphasis will be on the minirelaxation technique and the reason it should be a part of every 30-Second Swing. In Chapter 9, we'll revisit the topic of relaxation to see how you can use the more comprehensive relaxation technique to lay down Tracks of Excellence, a staple of running your brain successfully.

THE MINIRELAXATION TECHNIQUE

Oxygen-rich air is the lifeblood of activity. The cells that make up our bodies are like a network of tiny factories whose job it is to produce energy. Basically, you're in the import-export business: oxygen is your standard import and carbon dioxide is your prime export. When business goes well, you're firing on all cylinders; when it goes poorly, and the exports pile up, it reverberates throughout the whole company. The mechanism for keeping your oxygen–carbon dioxide exchange rates in balance is called breathing and you would think that because it's so important, we'd all be experts at it. Surprisingly, this is not always the case. Sometimes, just when you need it most, you don't breathe very efficiently.

How Good Are You at Breathing?

Under stress many people breathe high in their upper chest, an inefficient technique that promotes a shallow inhale and rapid breaths. In the extreme, it causes hyperventilation, a dangerous condition where there is a poor exchange between carbon dioxide and oxygen.

Contrary to popular belief, it is your cells, not your lungs, which regulate the rate of breathing. Tissue cells closely monitor the level of potentially dangerous carbon dioxide, and they are sensitive to the slightest increase or decrease. Thus when carbon dioxide levels drop, your breathing slows and, under some conditions, can stop completely. Mouth-to-mouth resuscitation works on this principle: to start a person breathing again, you blow your carbon dioxide into the other person's system. With the carbon dioxide levels rising, your cells signal the brain to increase the rate of breathing.

When you breathe too quickly under stress, you exhale too much carbon dioxide. This creates an oxygen–carbon dioxide imbalance that can cause a number of uncomfortable symptoms, including sweating, nervousness, tingling of the extremities, dizziness, anxiety, and even panic attacks—none of which is helpful to your golf game.

In addition to correct breathing, you can slow your heart rate by massaging a pressure point in your neck located below the earlobe and level with your jaw. This simple technique can calm you down under the pressure of a hard shot, or the emotional anxiety of a difficult round.

For the Power of Imagery to be available, the brain needs a steady supply of oxygen, yet under stress, access to full breathing capacity can drop to as low as 20 percent. It's obvious that the more efficiently you breathe, the more you can relax and that this state of relaxation gives you access to your Power of Imagery.

Triggering the Minirelaxation Technique

To trigger the minirelaxation technique you must breathe correctly, deep down in your abdominal cavity. Place your hand over your stomach, take a deep breath, and watch your belly swell and push your hand outward. Without releasing the air in your stomach, continue to fill your chest cavity with air. With both your abdominal and chest cavities filled with air, you are approaching your optimal volume—the total number of cubic centimeters possible in a breath.

Now reverse the process. Starting with your chest cavity, exhale until your belly has forced out all its air. After just one breath, you will feel a wave of relaxation sweep over you. That is a minirelaxation response and it keeps your mental screen liquid by staving off the flood of chemicals that come from the fight/flight response.

Another way to produce a modified relaxation response is to close your eyes, look upward behind your eyelids at about a 20-degree angle, and then breathe as above. You can do this on airplanes, at the office, or riding in the golf cart.

THE BONEHEAD EFFECT

Strange things can happen when you're under stress. One day I was late for an important meeting. I rushed out the door with the trash in one hand and my briefcase in the other. I hurried to the trash bin, threw in my briefcase, hopped into my car, and set the trash bag neatly on the passenger seat. Then I realized what I had done. This type of behavior, known as the "bonehead effect," most often occurs in extreme pressure situations when the ability to kick a short field goal in the waning moments of the Super Bowl or field an easy grounder in the deciding game of the World Series suddenly disappears.

The bonehead effect is evident in intellectual as well as physical tasks. Research shows that high concentrations of a hormone called cortisol, secreted by the adrenal gland, is present during stress, and this can disrupt intellectual functions and therefore affect physical performance. This is a double whammy for your golf game because, under stress, the following sequence can occur: you make a bad plan with faulty calculations (analytical), perform poorly (physical), then you immortalize the event by getting mad (emotional).

Jean Van de Velde's performance on the last hole of the 1999 British Open is a stellar example of the bonehead effect—a hangman's noose of bad decisions drawn ever more tightly by a cascade of poor execution.

Van de Velde, a relatively unknown European Tour player, was leading the Open by three shots with one hole to play. Under tremendous stress and in the clutches of the fight/flight response, Van de Velde made a huge mental error on the 18th tee. Despite water that snaked its way dangerously close to the right side of the landing area, he chose to hit driver. Van de Velde could have hit three successive seven-irons and easily won the British Open with a safe bogey but he chose the driver anyway. He hit the ball so far right that it cleared the water, a hazard positioned to catch only a moderately bad shot.

With a poor plan, a wild shot, and a narrow escape fresh on his mind, Van de Velde now faced his second shot. With an odd angle to the green, he made another terrible decision to go for it with a two-iron from an iffy lie, a plan that featured a long carry over water. He pushed that shot, the ball hit the grandstands and bounced back toward him into tall grass. His next shot found the water fronting the green, where the ball was visible but completely submerged. The entire viewing audience watched in amazement as he considered trying to play the submerged ball.

The television camera captured Van de Velde's puzzled how-did-I-get-here? look as he stood barefoot and bare-calved, knee-deep in his self-made watery grave. The crowd jostled for position so as not to miss the next act of what was turning out to be the greatest debacle in golf history.

In the end, Van de Velde triple bogeyed the last hole, and later lost a playoff to Scotsman Paul Lowery, who earlier had taken off his golf shoes too, but only because he was sure that his day was finished. The bonehead effect, empowered by stress run amok, had claimed another victim.

CONCLUSION

Having established the Power of Imagery, it follows that your golf game will be no better than your images of what your golf game should be. Note that there is no emphasis on swing mechanics. You have already learned your swing, even if it's imperfect, and it is now part of your unconscious competence. To play your best, you have to forget what you've learned about swing technique and play the game using the Power of Imagery to cue each swing. *There are some things in life that you can't think about while you do them, and golf is one of them.* Your swing mechanics are important—when you practice your swing—but when you're on the course you need to have some selective amnesia. This is one of the most difficult parts of becoming a champion because you have invested so much time and energy in learning your swing but *the game is not played the way it's learned*. There is an essential transition that you must make when the time is right—when you have imprinted "my golf swing" in your brain—a shift from mechanics to target; from the pieces of your swing to the holistic images that allow you to play your best golf.

IMAGES, NOT ANALYSIS

You should develop overall images that explain to your brain what you are trying to do with your swing. Remember that you are designed for success and your brain is a problem-solving behemoth that uses images as tools, so give your brain the tools it needs by becoming a master at feeding it images.

You should develop your own image repertoire for each part of your golf swing in order to unite golf and golf swing. Images are the form and golf swing is the substance. As examples, here are two swing images that will give you an idea of what an image looks like and how complete your images should be.

Image 1: The Release
A horse and rider are moving away from a wall with one end of a 60-foot rope tied to the saddle and the other end anchored inextricably to the wall. The horse gains speed and the rope rapidly uncoils until, in a bone-jarring tug, the rope goes taught and the horse stops dead in its tracks. As you can imagine, the rider is flung from the saddle in the direction that he and his horse were traveling together as a unit only a millisecond before.

Now let's reverse the situation so that our horse and rider are approaching a 6-foot wall at full gallop and, just as they get to the wall, the horse stops dead. Again, our hapless rider continues on as he's thrown over the wall.

COM

Both instances are an enactment of the Conservation of Momentum, a principle of physics that can be translated for our purposes as follows. A system (in this case the horse and rider) tries to hold on to its motion (its energy). When a segment or part of a system is slowed, the next segment attempts to pick up its motion, that is, to conserve the energy of the system. This is why a towel snaps, why a whip cracks, and why you should wear a seat belt.

You can now forget the physics concepts but keep in mind the image of passing along energy because this is how you build up, transmit, and deliver your power to the ball. In the first image, the wall represents your back leg. The second wall of your golf swing is your front leg. The rider is your club head and his separation from the horse is the release of your club head through the hitting zone.

This is an important concept that will allow you a nonmanipulative hand action throughout your swing so you can create power and accuracy without effort. Given the establishment of the wall, you don't "do" a release, you "have" one.

Image 2: How to Produce Power

The image is one of a generating station located on the outskirts of town, where big turbines produce the town's electrical power. Once generated, the power must be transmitted down the power lines until it arrives at its destination and is delivered for use.

The role of the turbines is played by the large muscles of your hips, back, and legs. When stretched by your coiling action, your muscles create energy, which translates into club head speed. It does this by passing from your power producing muscles, through your shoulders, down your arms, into your hands, down the shaft (the power lines), until finally the energy is emptied into the club head and applied to the ball.

If at any point in this three-phase representation of the golf swing there is an interruption, then power leaks develop. If you fail to coil, you won't have much power to transmit. If you fail to create leverage, your power will not be multiplied nor will your club return to impact correctly producing off-center hits and misdirected shots. If your sequence of motion is fouled so that your club head moves out and around to start your downswing rather than down and around, then your transmission lines are leaking.

Once your golf swing becomes automatic, these are the types of images that will guarantee you access to it.

CHAPTER 7

The Rehearsal

How many [swing thoughts] you can focus on depends on your levels of skill and concentration. On average I'd say that two is about the handicap golfer's limit and that he's better off most of the time with only one key swing thought. I must stress however that no matter how many things you think about at address, you are so to speak merely programming the computer. Once you throw the switch the computer must take over. The golf swing happens far too fast for you to consciously direct your muscles.

—JACK NICKLAUS

THE FULL-BLOWN DRESS REHEARSAL

ALL GREAT PLAYERS have rock-solid shot patterns they follow, an important part of which is their rehearsal swing. A few

Tomasi demonstrating the rehearsal

years ago, I was a spectator at the Masters looking back up the 15th fairway from the 16th tee. I saw Davis Love III about to hit his approach shot from the middle of the 15th fairway, a shot of about 195 yards. He made what looked to be a perfect swing, full and flowing, but I didn't hear anything or see a ball land on the green. Then I realized it was his practice swing, but it looked real enough to fool me. I thought to myself then, What an advantage to have, in effect, a legal mulligan on every shot.

In the previous chapters, you learned about making a shot plan that involves multisensorial images, where you see, feel, and hear the shot you are about to hit. At this stage in the 30-Second Swing, it's time to combine all those elements into an actual swing, the only difference being that you *image* the ball being struck instead of actually making contact. This is usually called a practice swing but that term can lead you astray.

One reason why practice swings are often ineffective is that most golfers leave both the ball and the target out of their rehearsal. If you're in the habit of leaving either of these out, you need to put them back in. Instead of a meaningless swing that bears no relationship to the plan, the target, or the ball, I want you to create a perfect replica of the actual swing you intend to make, complete with all the elements and sensations that are a part of your real swing, including imaging ball contact and ball fight.

This full-blown dress rehearsal provides a powerful link to the target that is a major contributor to generating your Go signal. By cueing your muscles, you are in effect priming the pump and, by actually imaging what you are about to do, your brain puts your whole body on alert. In effect, your mental command post says that there is a golf shot on the runway, clearance has been granted, and you are about to taxi into position for takeoff with all systems focused on the task at hand.

THE THREE ELEMENTS OF A PERFECT REHEARSAL

First, always take the same number of rehearsals for every shot—doing the same thing each time is what makes a routine *routine*. It's best to limit yourself to one rehearsal, with a second only if the first is not satisfactory. I'll promise you this, if you take three or more rehearsal swings, two things will happen. First, you'll be worn out before the end of your round and, second, you'll have difficulty finding people who will play with you.

An exception to the rule of one rehearsal swing is when you're faced with a specialty shot, such as an awkward lie. In this case, you need to give your brain a detailed map of the terrain and what it will take to negotiate it. Under these circumstances, you'll see expert players getting the feel for the shot by making a number of rehearsal swings, some very different from others. These kinesthetic auditions allow you to fit your feel to your eye and create a Go signal.

The other exception is when you make your rehearsal swing and it's a total flop. Say you usually take one practice swing that clips the grass perfectly but, on this occasion, something goes haywire and you accidentally dig up a big chunk of turf. There is no way that you can receive permission to make a good swing based on that rehearsal. In order to generate your Go signal, take a second rehearsal swing with total concentration on what your perfect swing feels like.

The second element of a perfect rehearsal relates back to imagery. Remember that images cue motor responses, so fill your brain with the image of your shot by rehearsing your swing in the direction of your target. If you rehearse hitting the ball toward the lake on the left or into the woods on the right, your brain receives the subtle message that you want your ball to go where your rehearsal is sending it.

It's a Package Deal

Third, be certain that you rehearse with good tempo, at the same swing speed necessary to send the ball to the target. Most good players have at least three speeds they use to create different kinds of shots with the same club. As part of your plan, you choose a swing speed and when you arrive at the rehearsal, you program in that speed (fast, medium, slow) so it's automatic in your actual swing.

Windshield Wipers

To understand how your golf swing can work at different speeds, image three settings for your windshield wipers. No matter what setting they're on, the wipers' speed is consistent with each sweep across your windshield, from slow back to slow through or fast back to fast through. The movement is symmetrical and framed in such perfect tempo that, after one or two passes, your eyes are no longer drawn to their action and you can concentrate on driving. Should a malfunction occur that causes one wiper blade to swing rapidly while the other lags behind, your eyes won't have a moment's rest.

Developing three speeds for each club is vital to becoming an accomplished player and you should work diligently in this regard. I suggest you do the following drill at the beginning and end of each practice session, remembering that good players normally swing at about 80 percent power, leaving 20 percent in reserve.

With a seven-iron, make three rehearsal swings. The first at a speed designed to hit the ball 50 percent of the normal distance; the second at the normal speed for a seven-iron; and the third at the speed that would sent the ball 20 percent longer than normal. Let's say you hit your normal seven-iron 150 yards. The goal for the first swing is a 75-yard seven-iron; for the second, 150 yards; and for the third, about 180 yards (it may not go that far but that is your goal). Now simply rotate the speeds until you can reproduce them on call.

ROTATION RATES

I use the term *rotation rates* to define the relationships of the parts of a golf swing, that is the chest, arms, hips, club head, etc., moving at different speeds but in exact relationship to one another. In a correct swing your chest, for example, moves at one speed, while your arms move at another speed. The key is that the ratio stays the same—they both speed up by the same increment when you want to hit the ball farther than normal.

> If, by mistake, you had a burst of arm speed, you'd ruin the relationship of your arms to your chest, making square contact impossible. You often see this mistake when the average golfer tries for the big hit and it becomes "all arms" from the top of the swing. It's not pretty to watch because your eye picks up the discord that is caused by disruption of the rotation rates. In contrast, when Tiger Woods puts it in high gear, *everything* moves faster, though the relationships stay the same. It is the same when Tiger, or any great player, hits a partial shot: everything moves slower, but no matter the speed, the rotation rates stay the same.

A book titled *It's the Damn Ball* by Ike Handy postulated that as soon as the ball is down there the swing goes from a syrupy smoothness to utter chaos. The good news is that with proper programming, you can maintain the swing speed you've chosen even with the "damn ball" in place. You just have to be sure that you sell your brain on the idea that each shot is a *package deal* involving two identical swings, one full dress rehearsal and one opening night. Note that I didn't say one swing is make-believe and one is real. Don't get in the habit of thinking that your rehearsal swing is just something you do before the real swing. Instead, make it so similar that you've "been there, done that" even before you've been there and done that.

Address Is No Place for an Audition

Other than programming in your swing speed, another advantage of a good rehearsal is that it is an opportunity to program in your swing thought or key. Waiting until you're over the ball, in your execution mode, is no place to audition swing mechanics. Once you're over the ball, you have to be operating under the auspices of unconscious competence, where you let habit prevail. To do this, you should have already decided who plays what role—and the place for that is the swing rehearsal. To repeat the quote at the beginning of this chapter, Jack Nicklaus said, "No matter how many things you think about at address, you are so to speak merely programming the computer. Once you throw the switch the computer must take over."

ABOUT SWING KEYS

I have said that there are some things in this life you shouldn't think about while you do them—walking, public speaking, romance, and golf come to mind, although not necessarily in that order. If you want to play your best, you can't think about a list of Things to Do while you swing. Many champions have one, maximum two, thoughts, that relate to their swing. These are termed swing keys in that they are thoughts that give you access to your complete swing, much as a key opens the door to where the valuables are kept. If the keys are well chosen, they represent your entire swing—a lifeline into your subconscious where the form of your golf swing is housed.

A good swing key gives you peace of mind—you know that if you follow its lead, success will result. If you use them correctly, swing keys will help you generate your Go signal. But swing keys aren't tips you hawk from one golfer or another. They are personal and while they work for you, they may not work for anyone else, which is why the same key may be the cure for one golfer and poison for another.

A Short Shelf Life

When you do find a swing key that complements your swing, don't be disappointed when the swing key works for a while and then fades away—that is the nature of swing keys. They are transitory, just-passing-through-type things, much like college dates—full of temporary commitments and fun while they last.

Still, used judiciously, swing keys are powerful tools, and if you can learn to select them carefully, it will help you to play your best golf. But be careful: there is no quicker way to ruin your swing than by tinkering with every key that catches your fancy. Here's how to handle swing keys.

First, try to choose swing mechanics that are already present in the pattern of your swing. For example, if you usually adopt a wide stance, you might focus on that as a key to help you maintain your overall golf balance. When that key loses its effectiveness, you might switch to keying on the one-piece takeaway you always use. Your brain will recognize these as old friends and it won't be confused when you reintroduce them into your conscious awareness.

Second, be sure the keys don't direct you to manipulate your swing in some way. Stay away from keys that tell you to do something or force something to happen. You want to let your swing happen, not make it happen. Swing keys become a problem only when you choose them haphazardly. Below are the distinctions you need to make in order to choose you keys well.

Two Types of Swing Keys

In order to select the right kind of key for a particular situation, you first must understand the two types of keys. An action swing key tells you to initiate a new move or establish a position. For example, "Roll the forearms through the ball" or "Fire your right knee." In contrast, a passive swing key tells you to maintain a position or continue a motion. For example, "Maintain spine angle" or "Let everything that's moving, keep moving."

Choosing a Swing Key

As a rule, the later in the swing you use an action key, the higher the risk that you will misapply it. The latest point where you can effectively use an action key is in the transition zone between backswing and downswing. Here a key such as "plant the left heel" can be very helpful. Whenever possible, try to choose keys that begin at address or during the takeaway. These are usually the most reliable and will continue to be effective the longest.

Avoid action keys during your downswing. Once you complete your backswing, it's too late to initiate any conscious moves before impact. It is inevitable that when you try to do "something" during the downswing (for example, arch your left wrist at impact or turn your right hip during the downswing), that "something" will occur at the wrong time and you'll foul the sequence of your swing. Remember that while our brain works fast, there is still a time lag between when an event happens and when we think it happens. This discrepancy means that our perception of the present is always wrong. The ball is a few yards down the fairway before the feeling of impact registers in our brain. Now, if we can't even tell accurately when the club makes contact, what chance do we have of trying to fit a set of conscious instructions into an event (the downswing) that takes less than half a second?

Action keys may work occasionally when your Time IQ is perfect but, because action keys are difficult to time correctly, they are more likely to produce a choppy, error-prone swing that results in inconsistent performances.

An exception: it's okay to use downswing action keys while working on a particular part of your swing *on the practice tee,* preferably under the supervision of a teacher. But once you're finished practicing the key, don't forget to put Humpty-Dumpty back together.

If you find you need a swing key during the downswing, make sure it's passive, one that tells you to hold a position or continue a motion. For example, "Keep the right heel down until it's pulled off the ground." This gives your swing an opportunity to unfold around a central theme that you establish before you begin your downswing.

As I outline in Chapter 5, make sure you have no "now" in your golf swing; no point at which you consciously try to hit the ball. A swing, by its nature, is a whole motion rather than "Swing," then

"Hit," then "Continue swing." If you have an identifiable feeling of hitting at a certain point in your swing, chances are you're using an action swing key that is causing you to manipulate the golf club.

WHY NO "NOW!"

Ben Hogan once commented that the downswing was no place to give yourself a lesson, and an experiment detailed in the instruction classic *Search for the Perfect Swing* proves Hogan's statement.

The researchers Alastair Cochran and John Stobbs placed golfers in a room with a single artificial light and had them hit drives into a net. Then they asked them to stop the swing as soon as they saw a light turn off.

Cochran and Stobbs described their research:

> The object of the experiment is to find out, by switching off the light at different points in the swing, at what stage the golfer is totally committed to his shot and quite unable to alter it in any way. Well, where would you say was the point of no return? . . . Of all the many golfers tested, not one could in any way alter his stroke when the light went off after a point just barely into the downswing. Nearly all could actually stop the shot if the light went out during the backswing.
>
> What this implies is that once any of us has fairly begun the forward swing, we can't correct or alter it in any way. This may surprise golfers. It didn't surprise the scientists carrying out the tests too much, because the time the downswing takes (0.2 to 0.25 seconds) is just about the minimum time required for the brain to perceive external signals, to give orders for the appropriate action, and for the muscles concerned to do something about it.

The message: since it physically can't be done, if you try to do something during the downswing, you will no doubt do it at the wrong time and ruin your swing.

DANGEROUS SWING KEYS

The distinction I make between active and passive swing keys assumes that the content of the swing key is correct but there are some keys you should avoid simply because they are poor advice or too easily misinterpreted.

While it's interesting to know what keys the great players use, many times they don't translate very well for you. Experts always have an unconscious sense of their swing that allows them to rotate swing keys, each of which helps to coordinate their over-all swing at the time. They don't change swings, they change keys; just as you don't change feet, you change socks. A new key promotes a synergism that can wake a swing from the dol-drums and, because it has the power of rejuvenation, it is often touted as being a golfing nonnegotiable—something everyone should do. Since it comes from a champion (or a champion's teacher or a TV infomercial that pays champions to say such things) it is received with open arms and immediately embraced by the golfing public. What has happened is a negotiable swing key has been sold as a nonnegotiable swing verity. And herein lies the snake in the snake oil: Where will you be when the swing key changes in a month and they don't notify you?

Another problem is that feel is a shaky edifice on which to build your golf swing. What champions feel they are doing and what they are actually doing are often at odds. When camcorders first came on the market, Al Geiberger used one to videotape his swing. Commenting on the experience, he said that he would make a change that felt dramatically different, yet when he looked at the video, the change was unnoticeable. Then he would exaggerate the change until it felt terrible, check out the tape, and still not be able to see anything. The point is that your feel can fool you, so when someone tells you about their latest secret move, treat it as a negotiable swing thought, not something around which you reconstruct your golf swing.

You can see the problems that can occur when you place all your hope on a heavily touted set of negotiable swing keys packaged up and sold to you as the Perfect Swing. If Moe does it, can the rest of the Stooges be far behind? You buy it, try it, it works for a while, then it's gone. All the while, *your* swing never improves, and your confidence erodes.

Throw Away These Keys

"Grip the club as if you were holding a little bird."

Not many people have ever held a little bird, and nobody has held one with the shape and weight of say a sand wedge. Besides which, if you are trying to hold on to a whirling object traveling at high speeds, the bird is a goner and rightly so.

"Let the club do the work."

If this is your key, you run the danger of producing a slow, powder-puff swing. That club of yours, regardless of what the infomercial says, is not some magical instrument. Stand the club in the corner and you will see that, by itself, it does no work at all.

"Keep your head still."

Tests show the head moves laterally in the good swing because, biomechanically, it has to. If you don't allow some movement, you'll hang on your left side and pick the club up steeply, plus you're liable to get a pain in the neck. While your head moves behind the ball before impact, it should never move past the ball toward the target until after the ball is on its way.

"Shift your weight."

There are pressure transfers in the good swing but thinking of shifting your weight leads to an overactive lower body that produces sliding instead of turning. This key evokes images of out-of-control cargo sliding around in the hold of a ship during a storm. When I ask a new student, who's lunging about, what he's trying to do, he'll invariably say, "I'm trying to shift my weight." Unfortunately, that's just what he's doing.

"Fire your right side."

This key causes most golfers to push up and off the right foot, thereby raising the body up and out of the shot. The right side needs to release as a result of being pulled around by the forces of the swing. It's a "let" rather than a "make." You let the right side rotate through the ball. Remember the Law of the Right Side—Let everything that's moving, keep moving.

"Turn your front shoulder under your chin."

This key is true but dangerously incomplete. Don't use the front shoulder as the benchmark of a good shoulder turn, because it can fool you. Humans can operate their shoulders independently, making it possible (and it often happens) that a golfer turns the front shoulder under the chin but shrugs the back shoulder upward, an incorrect motion that cuts coil and robs him of swing width.

"Pull down with the left hand" (right-handed players).

This swing key comes with the image of pulling on a bell rope. It's a great way to fade or in most cases slice the ball, because if you pull hard enough, you will prevent forearm rotation and leave the club face open at impact.

SUMMARY: IS IT REAL OR IS IT MEMOREX?

Your goal is to pull off the rehearsal of your shot so perfectly that your brain can't tell the difference between your rehearsal and your actual swing. In the next chapter, we'll explore the role of balance in your actual swing, but it is important that you introduce the form of balance during your rehearsal. If you repeatedly impose the form of balance on your swing action, the individual pieces of your swing will organize themselves into a functional unit around this form.

Give me a beginner hitting bad shots in perfect balance and, if you come back in a few months, I will show you a novice golfer who is hitting good golf shots in perfect balance. Such is the power of balance as an organizing principle—achieve the form and the substance will fill in.

So my advice is to program balance into your rehearsal by making it your goal to finish your "first swing" in perfect balance. When you finish in the correct position, it more often than not means you made the right moves along the way. Focusing on your follow-through programs the concept that your swing functions in perfect balance from the setup to the finish position.

The Pose

The finish of your swing is the conclusion of the follow-through, which I call the Pose, because you can hold it until the ball lands. A well-executed rehearsal for a regular full swing features a follow-through where the head, chest, and hips face the target and all of your weight is on your front foot. Your back foot is almost completely off the ground, with the toe of your back shoe serving as a balance point on the ground. A pose is a result, but if you train yourself to go to that position, you'll improve the earlier parts of your swing. When you know where you're going, you'll use the proper muscles and motions to take you there. So if you finish incorrectly, take a moment to stand in the correct follow-through position and concentrate on getting to this position—then redo your rehearsal.

Check that you have these four hallmarks of a well-balanced finish.

1. Your full body weight is on your front side.
2. You're standing at your full height.
3. The front of your body, including your back knee, is pointing in the direction of the target.
4. You're on your back toe, using your back foot as a balance point.

CHAPTER 8

The Commitment Line

The hen is involved; the pig is committed.
(On the contribution of each to the breakfast ham
and eggs.)

THE AVALANCHE: PLAYING FROM SLOW TO FAST

ONCE YOU'VE CONDUCTED a prefect rehearsal, your preparation is complete and the flow of your 30-Second Swing becomes like an avalanche carrying you to the ball. There was never a champion who just wandered up to the ball and hit it, but no one gathers a more powerful head of steam than Greg Norman did when he was playing his best in the late 1980s and early 1990s. Norman reminded me of a Doberman straining against a leash that must ultimately release him to tear at the ball.

While this burst of aggressiveness will not suit everyone, it does epitomize an avalanche. From behind the ball it slowly

Tomasi demonstrating the Commitment Line

builds while you're processing the information needed to develop a plan. As you approach the ball the pace begins to quicken. Once you reach the ball, you spend just enough time to confirm your Go signal. *The average player spends far too much time over the golf ball and not enough time behind the golf ball. The average player plays from fast to slow with no commitment. The good player plays from slow to fast with total commitment.*

Even a golfer as great as Greg Norman has problems when he loses his commitment and begins to doubt himself, and nowhere was it more evident than at the 1996 Masters. "His routine is so different," said David Leadbetter, referring to Greg Norman's behavior in his disastrous final round of the 1996 Masters. "He's standing over the ball an incredible amount of time. I'd say he's spending six, seven seconds longer per shot, fidgeting, moving around in ways I've never seen him do."

FULL COMMITMENT IS THE GOAL

The purpose of the steps you have already gone through (making a plan, relaxation, imaging, and a full dress rehearsal) is to generate full commitment to the shot you are about to play. You make a covenant with yourself—a promise that you will not deviate from the plan—and, in doing so, you consign all your resources to the task at hand. If you accomplish this total mobilization of resources on every shot for the rest of your golfing life, you would play to your potential all the time, which is all you can ask of yourself. We don't all have the same golf talent, but our assets can be allocated so that we make the most of what we have—and the way to do this is to be totally committed to every shot.

But, as you learned in Chapter 5, most golfers fail because they don't have the shot they are about to play clear in their mind. With a fuzzy set of instructions, your brain is a poor commander in directing your army of muscles to swing the club correctly.

In fact, it is commitment that separates the three levels of golfers—those who can't play, those who can play sometimes (usually when there is no pressure), and those who can play no matter what's at stake. Most golfers lack commitment to the shot and, with no clear purpose in mind, the ball can go anywhere— and often does. The good player is committed to the shot before he hits it but sometimes loses his commitment in midswing. The great player, unless his warning system gives a No signal, keeps his commitment to the shot plan from start to finish.

Commitment Leads to Closure

Besides the focus of resources, carrying out a commitment gives a sense of accomplishment, of closure, and that is important in keeping the hounds of self-recrimination at bay. If you fail under the auspices of full commitment, perfect permission, and a flow of Go signals, you can say to yourself (and yourself will listen), "I did everything I could—I gave it my best, yet it didn't work out, so it's on to the next shot." This act of closure keeps you on an even keel, safe from the stress chemicals that would flood you if you were to become angry with yourself for a less-than-perfect shot. When fate cheats you with a bad bounce, that's one thing; when you cheat yourself because you didn't give it your best, that is quite another.

There are several ways to generate commitment. One way is to use images that are so compelling that they rivet your attention to your plan. Another way to create commitment is to make a perfect rehearsal so your brain knows exactly what's expected of it. All of this takes place behind a line that separates you and the ball called the Commitment Line, or C-Line for short.

THE COMMITMENT LINE

As you look down your target line, imagine a line drawn perpendicular to the target line between you and the ball. This is your Commitment Line, and it represents a powerful part of your 30-Second Swing. You'll endow this invisible barrier with the magical power to turn you away at its border unless you are 100 percent committed to the shot you are about to play.

It's Not Your Rubicon

Though the C-Line shouldn't be crossed without total commitment to the shot, it is not the equivalent of Caesar's crossing the Rubicon where the die was irrevocably cast. Once you cross the C-Line you *can* turn back. In fact, a great player won't hesitate to retrace his or her steps back behind the C-Line to begin the routine again if a No signal pops up. And it is not unusual, especially under the pressure of an important shot, to start the avalanche in a state of Go, and somewhere along the way receive a loud No signal, in many cases while you're over the ball. When this happens, simply begin your 30-Second Swing again. Billy Casper, fifth on the all-time win list with fifty-five PGA Tour victories, would actually put the club back in his golf bag to start his routine over again—even if he wasn't going to change clubs. This is the pattern of a champion running his own brain.

CAN YOU RELOAD?

As we have already seen, converting a No signal to a Go signal is a three-step process. First you have to recognize that you're receiving a No signal. Second, you must go back behind the C-Line and start your routine again, and finally, you have to make the change that will generate a Go signal. It may seem odd, but the hardest part for most players is backing off the ball and reestablishing commitment. Even champions have trouble with this when they are not running their brain well.

Perhaps backing off is hard because the time it takes you to pull the trigger is so ingrained that you resist adding to it. Or maybe it's hubris, the false pride that persuades you to play through No signals. Or it could be that you're playing What Will People Think of Me? and you're concerned that your delay will make them think ill of you. Whatever the reason, you should realize that when you lose your commitment you lose permission; lose permission and you lose your focus; lose focus and your body systems are not all on the same page. When this happens, anarchy reigns. So whatever it is that tempts you to ignore the No signal, ignore the temptation instead. When you lose your commitment, make it your rule to head back behind the C-Line.

AIM, THEN ALIGN

Once across the C-Line your next step is to aim the club face at the target and then align your body to the club face. Whatever else golf is, it is a game of geometry—lines, angles, distances, and arcs that relate you, the club, your target, and the ball. Problem is, about 90 percent of amateur golfers misaim the club face to the right (for right-handed players).

Misaiming occurs when you approach the ball from the side. Because we have two eyes separated by a nose, trying to sight the target from this oblique angle distorts your vision and therefore your ability to locate the target. To avoid this, stand directly behind the ball and choose an intermediate target, a procedure that allows you to secure a far more accurate fix on the target's location. (See the four-target system outlined on page 165.)

The other reason so many golfers misaim is that when they practice, they rake balls from a pile to their right, without lining up each shot. Then, rather than hit out of the divot they just made, they move the ball to a slightly different position. A few balls later they are misaimed, but they don't realize or see their error because of their position beside the target line. After a few practice sessions, being perfect learners, they learn to aim "perfectly wrong" every time.

The Backward Evaluation System

Trouble is, once your club face aims away from the target, only a manipulation can square it to the target by impact. Without realizing it, you might close the club face (the compensation for a misaim to the right at address) or come over the top during the swing to make the club face point at the target at impact.

So when you're misaimed, the only way to hit a good shot is to make a bad swing. If you make a good swing, one without compensations, you'll hit the shot right of the target, in other words, make a bad shot. Misaiming introduces a backward feedback system where good swing = bad shot (a bad result), and bad swing (if you come over it just enough) = good shot.

You couldn't learn anything with this Mad Hatter feedback system—where good is bad and bad is good—and golf is no exception. To play your best and preserve your golf swing, you must be sure you're aimed and aligned perfectly for each shot, both in practice and on the course, and the only way to do this is to make correct aim and alignment part of your 30-Second Swing.

Here is a poem I recite to students who misaim. Its author, for obvious reasons, has chosen to remain anonymous.

My golf swing used to leave me, it would vanish overnight.
I knew I had a problem and it made me so uptight.
But now I've solved my problem, I've finally seen the light;
It wasn't lack of talent, I was aiming too far right.

Sam Snead is but one example of a fine player who aimed to the right and hit the ball superbly (and some great ones aim left). But the small percentage of elite players who vary from the norm do so only slightly and they understand exactly what they are doing. It's a different story for the average player who unwittingly aims so far right that it compromises his chances of developing a sound swing and playing his best golf.

THE GOOD GOLF EQUATION: GOOD GOLF = GOOD DIRECTION + GOOD DISTANCE

Direction is determined by your address position, leaving you free to concentrate on producing the correct distance, a task that you have mostly completed by selecting the correct club and cueing your swing speed during your rehearsal.

FIRST TAKE CARE OF DIRECTION

Establish direction by selecting your target line, intermediate marker, and landing area as you make your plan from behind the ball. As you address the ball, first sole your club behind it and aim the club face, guided by your intermediate marker, in the direction that you want the ball to start. Then build your setup around the club face by stepping into position without moving the club head so that your body is perpendicular to the club face. If you drew a line connecting your feet it would be essentially parallel to the target line and it would be perpendicular to a line extending from the bottom edge of the club face.

It is essential that you establish your direction with the correct geography at address. *Never try to create the direction of your golf shot with your golf swing.* Knowing that your direction is set at address will go a long way in producing your total commitment to the shot.

THE FOUR-TARGET SYSTEM

Golf is basically a seek-and-find-the-target game and, as Harvey Penick said, you need to "take dead aim." To help you pinpoint your target, use a four-point reference system that takes advantage of the way your eyes naturally gauge distance and direction.

Once you have a clear image of your shot, pick a main target where you want the ball to finish. Then pick a marker in the distance behind your main target—a tree, fence post, bunker, or rooftop—in line with it. If you identify only the main target—a patch of grass up to several hundred yards away—you run the risk of losing it when you look away to address the ball. Draw an imaginary line back from your distant target, through the main target, and back to the front of the ball. Now, pick out a close or intermediate target on that line—a divot, old tee, or some other mark. Your immediate target is the ball.

As you take your address position, set the club face behind the ball square to your intermediate target and then set your body square to the club face. Some players, like Jack Nicklaus, use an intermediate target that's about 12 inches in front of the ball; others, like Greg Norman, use one that's 30 feet ahead. In either case, you can more accurately aim the club face at an object near to you than one that's far away, making the intermediate target a valuable reference point. When you look out from your setup position to confirm your main target, you'll recognize it immediately with the help of your more obvious distant target, as well as your intermediate target.

The Procedure

1. Pick your main target from behind the ball.

2. Approach the ball and position the club head directly behind it before you assume your golf posture. Point the aiming lines on the heel and toe of your club face at your intermediate target. Taking your stance before you aim your club face is a major cause of misaiming.

3. Once your club is soled, align your shoulders, hips, and feet to the target line in the manner that suits your swing–body type matchup (some players are slightly open, some slightly closed while most position their body square to the target line). Take great care not to dislodge the aim of your club head while you are assuming your golf posture.

Tomasi demonstrating the procedure

4. Mentally connect the targets by drawing a line that starts at the ball (T1), extends through the intermediate target (T2) and through the main target (T3), and ends at the distant target (T4).

The Distance Fix

With full commitment, you're in your address position and you're ready to execute your shot. You have taken care of direction with your setup and distance with your club selection and rehearsal swing speed. At this point you look at the target for your final distance fix. You're not recalculating but simply reconfirming the target's location as the last step before you slide into execution mode.

What happens next depends on the individual. Some golfers receive their final Go signal by running through a checklist—for example, they make sure their feet, hips, and shoulders are correctly positioned. One of my students, a surgeon, appeared to fidget at address before he started his swing. Although he is a very good player, he was self-conscious about the amount of time he spent over the ball and his worry about what other people were thinking of him was producing a big No signal.

AUDITORIES TALK

As an auditory, the doctor was silently reciting an extensive checklist in his mind, just as he did to prepare for an operation. While his meticulous preparation for surgery gave him permission to succeed, the same kind of procedure produced the opposite result in golf. The solution was not to stop using a verbal checklist—that was the way he received his Go signal—it was simply to pare down the number of items on that list to decrease his time over the ball.

KINESTHETICS FEEL

Verbal checklists aren't for everyone. Golfers who are kinesthetic have a feeling that things are, or are not, all in their proper place. For these golfers, there are no pictures or checklists at this stage. For example, another of my students, a professional golfer, was having trouble with his pitch shots. Mike is a large, powerful man who hits the ball a long way off the tree. I watched him pitch about twenty balls using decent technique, and noticed that the five shots he hit poorly included a preswing stutter step at address that was absent in his normal routine. I asked him about it and he said that he didn't feel comfortable over those shots but he wasn't exactly sure why. Basically he was getting a No signal that manifested itself in the form of a physical movement.

We worked on having him honor the kinesthetic No signal by restarting his 30-Second Swing each time he received the message. When he did, his pitching improved. A few lessons later, dramatic improvement occurred when we found the root of the No signal. He revealed that he wanted to hit the ball farther than anyone else off the tee. His concept of golf was that anyone could chip, pitch, and putt (he wasn't a great putter either), but only a few players could hit a ball 300-plus yards.

Mike's entire golf identity was built around his hidden agenda (hidden from himself) to be the longest hitter, and he had several Long Drive titles to prove it. Consequently he rarely practiced his short game. Once his agenda changed from long ball to low score, not only did his pitching improve but so did his entire short game. The improvement was so dramatic that he qualified to play in his first Tour event shortly thereafter.

VISUALS SEE

At this point in the 30-Second Swing—just before the club starts away from the ball—visual types are making pictures. Many visuals are sensitive to light changes, especially on partly cloudy days where the sun peeks in and out. I was on the course with one of my players when a problem that always mystified her reared its ugly head. Terry would be playing along quite nicely and suddenly, just before she swung, she'd receive an inexplicable No signal that resulted in a fat shot.

On this day, Terry was playing well and had hit a big drive that left her a pitching wedge to the green. It was a typical windy

Florida day where puffy, fast-moving clouds periodically turned the brilliant sunlight on and off. I noticed that a second before she started the club back, a cloud blocked the sun and the light changed dramatically. Sure enough, she hit behind the ball, leaving it well short of the green. The change in lighting was enough to distract this visually oriented player and, armed with this knowledge, she now knows to restart her 30-Second Swing when this happens just before she swings. To take even more control of the situation, Terry now checks the cloud movement in the planning stage of her 30-Second Swing, which also helps her better gauge the wind.

INVEST IN YOUR IRA

When you look back to the ball just before you start your swing, your visual lock on the target is broken. Your visual focus then moves to the ball, and the longer you stare at it, the dimmer your visual memory of the target becomes. When your visual fix on the target is broken, you switch to your sense of feel to guide the rest of your golf swing. This sudden switch from visual to kinesthetic can be troublesome, especially under pressure. Your Image Retention Ability (IRA) is a skill that allows you to maintain your visual lock on the target even when you're not looking directly at it, and it is a skill that you can improve even if the visual is not your dominant sense.

To understand your Image Retention Ability, try this experiment. Stare at a nearby object for a few seconds—a doorknob, for instance. Close your eyes and you should find the object's afterimage on your mental screen. At first you may only be able to see its shape for a brief instant, but as you improve your image retention skills, you'll be able to hold a clear image of your target on your screen for several seconds or more. Your goal is to hold the target image long enough for it to cue your golf swing.

Increasing Your IRA

Focus and practice can increase your IRA. Focusing brings the object into clear, detailed view on your mental screen—you want to see the flag, its color, the flagstick, where it is on the green, the green's contour, and all other relevant elements of the target.

To develop focus, try to hold the shape of the object on your afterimage screen; then hold the color, then progressively add particulars until your focus is complete and the object is perfectly captured as an afterimage on your screen. It may take you a week or two, or you may be able to do it after a couple of tries, but once you can hold a focused afterimage for several seconds, you're ready to go outside and practice.

The second way to increase your IRA is with outdoor practice. Use the technique for every shot on the range, on the golf course, and especially on the putting green. Soon you'll be able to look at the target, then look back at the ball and make your swing with a clear afterimage of the target as your swing guide.

THE SWING TRIGGER

Once you have aimed the club face and then aligned your body to it, you need a transition move that starts your swing. The term *waggle,* as it is commonly used, is too restrictive in describing this move. I prefer the term *trigger,* a movement repeated for each shot that accompanies your Go signal. A good trigger is a bridge connecting your preswing preparation to your in-swing action—a seamless transition from one to the other that comes in many forms. Lee Trevino shuffles his feet in perfect rhythm. Many players press their hands slightly toward the target. Others, most notably Gary Player, press their back knee toward the target. Then there is the barely perceptible weight-rock, where a player shuttles his weight from one foot to the other. The most prevalent trigger is the swishing back and forth of the club using the wrists and arms, à la Ben Hogan, who made the trigger a science.

Jack Nicklaus's head rotation is surely the most famous of triggers. "I had used what I call a 'stationary press,'" Nicklaus explains in *Golf My Way.* "It was simply an increase of hand pressure on the shaft, a firming up of the grip just before I started the club away from the ball. . . . I combined this with a movement common to many tour professionals, and particularly pronounced in Sam Snead. Just before we start back, Sam and I very noticeably swivel our chins to the right."

From Ball on the Ground to Ball in the Air

It doesn't matter how you receive your Go signal—feel it, see it, hear it—one way is no better than another—but once the Go is on, your swing begins, marking the final stage of the avalanche, and the end point in the flow to Go. The result: ball in the air.

THE LOST-COMMITMENT BOGEY

Accomplished players don't try to manipulate the club very often, but occasionally it happens to the best players in the world, thanks to loss of commitment. You feel like you're going to hit a good shot, you have a Go signal because you have the shot in your repertoire and you've made a good plan. You cross the Commitment Line in an avalanche, feel good over the ball, and then hit a less-than-great shot. The cause may be what I call the lost-commitment bogey.

Case in point: With water to the left of the green and the pin tucked to the right, it is easy to make a plan to start the ball between the water and the flag and fade the ball into the pin. And as part of your 30-Second Swing, you know you should fade the ball with your setup and not your swing. This is all well and good before you start the club in motion but if, during your swing, you lose your commitment and you cut it by manipulating your swing in some way (perhaps holding the blade open just a bit), you'll overdo the fade. This loss of commitment leaves you on the short side of the pin facing a tough up-and-down.

You pay the price for losing commitment *during your swing* with exasperating lapses that are hard to understand. Worse yet, it can give you the impression that a bad shot can pop up anytime and for no reason, even if you have done everything you are supposed to do. If you don't understand the root cause, over time it will undermine your confidence. If taken to an extreme, it suggests that you are a choker or that you always find a way to lose.

The irony of the lost-commitment bogey is that, since its true cause isn't apparent, there's a danger that you'll interpret it as a swing problem. Then you go back to the range to work on your fade when you really should be working on the grand finale of your 30-Second Swing—keeping your commitment from start to finish.

A TWO-HANDICAP HOMUNCULUS?

In the previous chapter, I stressed that if you clearly defined the form of what you want your golf swing to be and continued to pursue it, the substance will fill in. The form is universal, while the substance is the particular expression of that form. Concepts are forms and it is my firm conviction that your golf swing will be no better than your concept of what a good golf swing is, which is a verbal tip of the hat to the power of the form to shape your golf swing.

It is this distinction between form and substance that explains why you can't reproduce your golf swing perfectly every time. Your brain doesn't store the actual substance of your swing—you have to re-create it with each swing by moving muscles and bones in certain ways through time and space. There is not a little man in your brain, a golfing homunculus with a Nike swoosh on his hat who makes a golf swing every time you want one.

What your brain stores is the form of your swing and then, with each swing, the substance—the actual movements—flows into the form. This is why your concepts about your golf swing must be clear. If your forms are fuzzy, how can you expect your swing mechanics to be correct? If mechanics take the shape of the form and the form is wrong, then your swing will never be strong enough to support your game.

When someone isn't playing well, British golf aficionados often say the player is "off form," which is an insightful description. The role of the 30-Second Swing is to bridge the gap between form and substance on every shot.

THREE BASIC FORMS THAT SHAPE YOUR SWING: TIME, SPACE, AND BALANCE

By now it is clear that the one and a half seconds it takes to make a golf swing is not the only thing in the 30 or so seconds it takes to prepare for and hit a golf shot. While this isn't a book about swing mechanics, it will certainly be helpful to explore the forms of time, space, and balance into which your individual swing mechanics must fit.

Form 1: Time

To swing the club correctly in the three spatial dimensions (height, width, and depth), you must control your sense of time, the sense I call Time IQ. The "commonsense" view of time is that it's incremental, absolute, uncontrollable, and therefore ultimately unmanageable. But is this really the case or can we control time by redoing our concept of it? Can time be personalized?

Personalized Time

There is a very important factor that can change time, and that is your perception. Pleasant experiences are over quickly, unpleasant ones seem to last forever. As Albert Einstein said, "Put your hand on a hot stove for a minute, and it seems like an hour. Sit with a pretty girl for an hour and it seems like a minute. That's relativity." And he should know!

The rate at which our lives flow by can change depending on whether we're looking forward or backward. Ask a fifty-year-old person how far away fifty seemed when he or she was twenty, and most say it seemed very far off; then ask them how long it took them to go from age twenty to fifty. "A blink of an eye," is the usual response.

When you can run your brain, time doesn't march on, speed up, or slow down, unless you tell it too. Many great athletes report the ability to make time stand still or at least to slow it dramatically while they are in competition. Former NBA star Bill Walton said, "Everything slows down. It's like everybody is wearing cement shoes, the ball is in slow motion, everything slows down except you, and you feel like you're operating at a different speed and at a different level than anybody else." Greg Norman's perception of time when he's playing well mirrors Walton's: "Everything goes by in slow motion," Norman says. "Your swing feels like it's in slow motion, it seems like you have all the time you need to make a decision."

Controlling Your Time IQ

Since the time dimension has a marked effect on the three spatial dimensions your club must pass through when you make a swing, fluctuations in your Time IQ are a common cause of swing problems. You rush to the course, hit a few shots that aren't satisfactory because your Time IQ is a little off, and immediately you make major swing changes to make the ball go straight. You fiddle with your grip, change your ball position, swing the club more outside—all this just five minutes before you tee off. As these changes mount, so does your brain's confusion, and finally your golf swing vanishes.

Thus, a vital part of learning and then keeping your golf swing is to understand your Time IQ, that is, your sense of time. In addition to understanding, you must also be able to recalibrate your built-in metronome when your timing is off.

How Your Time IQ Is Established in Your Golf Swing

How does your brain know how long your swing takes? If you let it, your brain measures the time in your golf swing as the interval between the first movement of the club away from the ball until the feel of impact. That interval is registered as "the time I have to swing the club," and it's no wonder you try to speed the club up because that's not much time (less than a second and a half) to make your swing. But you can give yourself the gift of time if, instead of the ball, your prime target is the place where you want the ball to end up. Your concept must be: *My golf swing runs from the beginning of my shot routine and ends when the ball is on the ground—some 30 to 45 seconds.*

The Gift of Time

It's your choice: You can change your golf swing by changing your concept of time. You can cut up your swing so that there's a *hit* in one segment or you can expand your swing time by thinking of your swing as a unity, a whole that includes what you do before, during, and after "the swing." You can look at time as a scarce commodity, one your golf swing uses up rapidly, or you can choose to perceive that you have all the time in the world to make a golf shot. A major part of running your brain involves how you handle time—it runs you or you run it—it's your choice.

Time Control Technique

To implant the image in your brain of you swinging the club with *all the time in the world*, videotape yourself hitting balls and then watch the tape over and over in slow motion, repeating one of the phrases below or one of your own. But be careful not to critique your golf swing. All you want is to link the visual image, your concept of time under control, and the verbal statement. When the three are merged into one image, the phrase will act as an anchor. When you repeat it as you play or practice, it will pull up what's attached to it—in this case, your golf swing with time under your control.

Here are sample anchor phrases that you can repeat as you watch your swing:

The Sweet Surrender to Gravity
No Ball Before Its Time
The Ball Is on the Arc, I Don't Have to Find It
Cultivate the Wait
Effortless Power, Not Powerless Effort
Passive Power
Finish High and Let It Fly
Give the Club Time to Change Directions
I Give Myself the Gift of Time
There Is No "Now" in My Swing
"Let" Rather Than "Make"
Time Is Mine
I Have All the Time in the World
I Control My Mind and My Time
My Time Is "My" Time

IT'S NINE O'CLOCK. DO YOU KNOW WHERE
YOUR HANDS ARE?
If you're like a lot of my students, when you're playing well, you think you'll never play badly again and when you're playing badly, you're certain you'll never play well again. Neither belief is true, of course, but it brings up an interesting ques-

tion: Why does your golf swing come and go on such a seemingly random basis? It appears to make no sense at all.

Part of the answer relates to "no sense," the failure of your brain to sense where your hands are after they leave your visual field. While you may not be consciously aware of it, your brain has no problem keeping track of your hands when they are in front of you because they are "seeable" either by looking directly at them at address or through your peripheral vision during the takeaway. And it is your hands, as the feel center of your swing, that allow you to track the club head—so you could say that your hands are the club head.

The Pass Along

But, during your backswing, as your hands approach nine o'clock, they leave your visual field and your brain must now rely solely on its network of sensors scattered throughout your body whose job it is to report what body parts are where.

Golf's "big three" are the ball, the target, and the club head, and since you don't look at either the target or the club head for the majority of every swing, you've lost visual contact with two of the big three. The problem is that when you suddenly deprive your brain of its dominant tracking system (sight), as you do at some point in every swing, it requires a smooth transition from your visual to your kinesthetic system—the pass-along—to keep the club head going where it should. *Turning over every swing to your sense of feel is just asking for trouble because, unless you practice or play every day, and are stress free and healthy as a horse, "feel" is a shaky edifice on which to build your swing.*

There are two steps you can take to keep your good swing around as long as possible. First make a blueprint of your good swing—write down, in detail, what you do when you are swinging well. It may sound simple, but even Jack Nicklaus has trouble doing it. He admits that when he discovers a swing key that works he often can't remember to use it the next day. He once told his caddie, "You've got to start writing these things down," and so do you. If you don't know what you're doing, see your teaching pro and write down what s/he tells you. With your blueprint in hand you quickly can reconstruct your swing when it starts to go south.

Second, do the following drill anytime your swing starts to go bad: Close your eyes and from your normal address position swing your hands to waist high. Now open your eyes and check how near you came; then adjust and close your eyes to fix the feel. Repeat this closed-open-adjust-closed sequence with your hands at nine o'clock, both for the backswing and the downswing. This will help you make the transition from sight to feel without a hitch for every swing.

Form 2: Space

As far as we know, everything we do in this universe, including playing golf, occurs in the four dimensions. By controlling your Time IQ, you learned how to deal with one dimension, and in this section you'll learn how to deal with the other three—height, width, and depth.

How you move your body around in space determines how well you'll satisfy the laws of physics at impact. Each body type fills space differently and thus has its own dominant dimension.

Three Body Types

In 1940, sociologist W. H. Sheldon created a scale that allowed a division of the general population into three prototypic body types, endomorph, mesomorph, and ectomorph. Within and across the three types, there is much variation when it comes to characteristics such as size, strength, flexibility, and bone structure, and it's these characteristics that determine, in large part, how you will swing a golf club.

Each body type has a dominant dimension (DD) and an accompanying dominant power source (DPS) in which your body functions most efficiently when making a golf swing. Thus the key to a good golf swing is to match your swing mechanics, such as grip, stance, and posture, to your body type, a matchup that will guarantee you access to your DD and its corresponding DPS.

It's Not Your Fault

Simple observation shows that some people are evenly proportioned, with wide shoulders and a medium-size skeletal frame. A well-conditioned mesomorph is muscular with a triangle-shaped upper body, while the average mesomorph is less defined with a little more body fat. These individuals should use the Leverage Swing. Other golfers have narrow chests with long angular features and high flexibility, and they are prototypical ectomorphs. This body type should adopt the Arc Swing. The third group has thick chests, limited flexibility, and often has short, powerful arms. They are power players who can use their muscles to good effect. This body type should use the Width Swing.

The three power sources and their dominant dimension (DD) are:

1. Arc, the distance and height the club head travels during the swing. The DD is height.

2. Leverage, the mechanical advantage derived from the arrangement of fulcrums and levers. The DD is depth.

3. Width, the swinging of the club away from the body, creating the widest possible arc, then delivering the club head back to the ball using the large muscles of the upper body. The DD is width.

You will fill in the form of space and play your best golf *when you identify your dominant power source and then adopt the swing mechanics that allow you to access your dominant dimension.*

Form 3: Balance

The balance system coordinates information from all the senses. Balance affects vision, touch, feel, rhythm, cadence, as well as your sense of time. But there is more to the form of balance than this physical system. Balance is an equilibrium that, if disturbed, causes a system such as the human body to act to regain its lost state. The balance system, therefore, has the power to direct movement—to initiate action. Balance is a symmetry of parts organized in harmony; disrupt it and the system can do nothing but use all of its energy to recover.

Two important characteristics of balance:

1. Balance is the organizing principle of a good swing. That is one reason you see swing differences ranging from Jim Furyk to Ernie Els, each unique, but all the parts organized within the form of balance.

2. Balance can be cultivated and you can put its organizational powers to work for you.

A Symmetry: When Golf Balance = Street Balance

Street Balance

Evolution has given you a balance system that, among other things, keeps you safe from falling. The physical part of this system is composed of tiny sensors located throughout your body, primarily in your muscles, joints, and the fluid in your inner ear. Your brain receives a continuous flow of information about the position of your body and gives orders to your muscles to regain your balance whenever your body is in danger of falling.

This unconscious self-preservation system is what I call street balance and, though it can save your life, it can also ruin your golf swing. Since remaining upright is vital to survival, your brain attaches high priority to any message that says, "This container is about to fall over." When it receives such a message, it automatically takes action to recover. This reflex is called the "righting instinct" and its power to control your body is supreme. Hit some ice while skiing and back on your heels you go; slip on a banana peel and out shoot your arms; trip over the rope that cordons off the green from golf carts, and you'll dance an inadvertent jig to regain your street balance.

Golf Balance

The contorted arrangements (spine tilted, body bowed, left side straight, right side flexed, head back, front hip ahead, etc.) involved in hitting a golf ball require *golf balance*. The key is to maintain these variations from the norm without triggering the righting instinct because, if you do, street balance will override golf balance every time. When it does, it will prevent you from arriving at impact in the posture necessary for good shot making. You won't fall down but you'll ruin your shot. To play your best golf, your street balance must equal your golf balance. Following are some essentials of golf balance.

Balance and Pressure Flow

Good golf balance involves the proper channeling of weight flow (load) into your hip joints—from the front hip to the back hip during your backswing and then from the back hip to the front hip during your downswing. Loading first one hip, then the other, at just the right time—a process I call the hip switch—keeps your body in perfect balance, a symmetry where your street balance equals your golf balance.

I define weight flow in terms of a pressure transfer. Thinking in terms of pressure cues the image of a stable lower body that provides a platform for the efficient energy flow necessary for a powerful swing. A correct pressure transfer is a subtle, almost covert transfer of loading one hip, then the other, all barely visible to the naked eye. This is in contrast to the image of weight shift, which raises the specter of major changes in position involving asymmetrical lunges and lurches, about as subtle as a loose cannon on deck in a storm.

Pressure Versus Weight—a Distinction

Pressure is how your weight is concentrated. A 175-pound man can walk across a green leaving only light tracks, yet a 100-pound boy hobbling across the same green on crutches would leave a trail of deep holes.

The pressure you exert (pounds per square inch) is a dynamic force—it changes depending on how you apply it. Weight is static. Your weight stays the same on earth no matter the configuration of your body—stranded on one leg, lying down, standing erect—your weight stays the same.

Pressure as it flows into joints causes load, and this load is how you apply pressure while you swing. In your golf swing, to satisfy the form of balance, you must transfer pressure, not weight.

Balance and Joint Alignment

An additional aspect of golf balance is the alignment of load-bearing joints, whose role it is to allow movement while providing maximum stability. When these joints are not in alignment they are not prepared to accept the transfer of load during the swing and they buckle under the pressure. This imbalance triggers the righting instinct.

Another Kind of Symmetry: Balance and Force

During the swing, the out-force tries to pull the club head away from the swing center while the in-force attempts to pull it back. If the out-force wins, an imbalance is created and the club effectively lengthens. Thus, the club head moves outside the correct return arc and a heeled shot results. If the in-force wins, the club effectively shortens, producing shots off the toe. A golfer who changes the effective length of the club in the up-down direction, hits thin shots by contacting the middle of the ball and fat shots (ground before ball) respectively. Keeping the forces described above in balance requires control of both space and time.

Still Another Kind of Symmetry: Balance and Time

As you have seen, your Time IQ includes calibrating the rate at which body parts move in relation to other body parts, for example, the right shoulder and right hip traveling at the same rate, though not the same speed. A movement, either overdone or underdone, imbalances both the rate and sequence of movement. What works in moderation is destructive in excess. If you overemphasize leg action, you risk leaving the upper body too far behind. Overemphasize your arm swing and the upper body takes over, freezing out the legs. In the process of learning the basic mechanics of the golf swing and maintaining them once they are in place, the golden mean (everything in moderation) is one of the most important moderators of golf balance.

CHAPTER 9

Tracks of Excellence

La Gorda and I used *dreaming together* as a means of reaching an unimagined world of hidden memories. *Dreaming together* enabled us to recollect events that we were incapable of retrieving with our everyday-life memory. When we rehashed those events in our waking hours, it triggered yet recollections that are more detailed. In this fashion, we disinterred, so to speak, masses of memories that had been buried in us. It took us almost two years of prodigious effort and concentration to arrive at a modicum of understanding of what had happened to us.

—CARLOS CASTANEDA, *The Eagle's Gift*

THE EVOLUTION PHASE

THE EVALUATION PHASE of the 30-Second Swing begins as you swing up and into your finish position. As soon as you see the

Tomasi demonstrating the evaluation phase

ball in the air, you begin monitoring its flight, ready to deal with the outcome, whatever it may be. If the outcome is good you'll emotionalize it; if it is bad, you'll acknowledge it, replay it in a practice swing, image the result you wanted, then emotionalize your imaginary outcome. To do this effectively you must understand how your emotional system works and how you can make it work for you.

THE PAST CONTROLS THE FUTURE, IF YOU LET IT

Have you ever watched someone hit a ball in the water and then you hit your ball in the water too? Have you ever waited patiently to roll in your 3-footer while another player lags a putt to 3 feet, decides to putt out, misses, and then so do you? In situations such as these, your swing mechanics don't let you down—you could have made that putt with your eyes closed—the problem is that bad memories are filling your mental screen and causing you to perform perfectly wrong.

If your practice-range performance is consistently better than your on-course performance, chances are you have a strong and compelling database of memories that are preventing you from playing your best golf. For you, bad on-course memories breed bad shots until playing poorly becomes a habit. Unfortunately, your Tracks of Failure—bad golf memories—are providing a blueprint for how to play your worst golf. To break the bad memories–bad shots cycle, it's helpful to know something about how those memories are laid down.

TRACKS OF EXCELLENCE AT WORK

Sporting a new hip as he arrived at the 2000 Masters, sixty-year-old Jack Nicklaus's game, by his own admission, was at its nadir. Nevertheless, until the bone-chilling wind blew them away in the third round, Jack Nicklaus relied on his Tracks of Excellence, accumulated over forty-one years of success and a record six wins at the Masters. This sixty-year-old man spent two rounds on the tournament leader board. At age fifty-eight, he had finished tied for sixth place and at age forty-eight became the oldest winner in Masters history. "I believe in myself when I play here," said Nicklaus. "I suppose Augusta brings out the best in me."

YOUR PAST INFLUENCES THE PRESENT

Your memories are stored in the neural networks of your brain and they are the basis for your internal narrative, of which you are the star. They serve as information upon which you base your assumptions, form perceptions, and ultimately choose how you respond to your environment. Thus, in an important way, the past influences the present, so it's wise to be careful what you put in your storage bin.

ALTERED PERCEPTION

In a classic behavioral science study, toddlers were put in a room with several harmless grass snakes. After a few minutes, the children were playing happily with the snakes and showed no fear whatsoever. Then their mothers were brought in and, when they saw their children playing with snakes, they frantically pulled the children away from the snakes and rushed them from the room. Sensing their mothers' horror, all the toddlers began to cry.

Afterward, when the toddlers were shown pictures of snakes, they reacted with fear and revulsion. The exact same stimulus—a snake—with a different meaning now, produced a different response.

THE BRAIN: IT'S ALL IN THERE

In the early 1950s, Dr. Wilder Penfield, a neurosurgeon, performed open-brain surgery on a female patient. Since there are no nerve endings in the brain, once the cranium is penetrated under local anesthesia, a patient can remain awake. Penfield found that when a particular part of the brain was stimulated, the woman had total recall of various experiences, complete with emotions.

One result of that initial discovery was that emotions (love, anger, hate, fear, etc.) are important ways of tagging experience. When you emotionalize an experience, it becomes significant to you, making it more likely that you will be able to recall the experience consciously at a later date.

In your database, experiences are stored in a hierarchy, from most important to least important, with your dominant, most emotionalized memories topping the charts. When it comes time to decide how to react to a current event, the relevant memories at the top of the hierarchy are jogged first. While the past is not so omnipotent that it condemns you to make the same mistakes time and again, its power to influence the present is not to be taken lightly.

Basically, unless there is a compelling reason not to, you will behave in the present as you did in the past. Consequently, your past has an inertia that can only be disrupted by an equal and opposite force, which is one reason change can be so difficult— it takes effort. The good news is that there is a way to channel your effort so you can create a better golf game, an explanation of which takes up the rest of this chapter.

The other general implication of Dr. Penfield's findings is that once an experience leaves short-term holding it moves into long-term memory, where it is permanently stored. Brain researcher, Dr. Michael Persinger, appearing on the television show *The Unexplained* (A&E network, June 2000) described his study of near death experiences (NDEs) and their relationship to the structure of the brain. He found that when he simulated the conditions of a near death experience by stimulating certain areas of the brain, he could reproduce the characteristics of the NDE, including the life review, which suggests that the events of your life are all permanently stored in your memory.

So despite the fact that you may not be able to recall them at will, all of your experiences reside in your subconscious brain. For the most part, unless there is injury to your brain, you never forget anything.

I've stated that playing the game well requires that you have access to your golf database—your ability to recall the form of your golf swing each time you play a shot. If there were no record of your swing, then each shot would be even more of an adventure than it is now. But the question in this chapter is not if there is a record of your golf game stored in your neural networks, that is a given. The question is, How is that record laid down and can you change it if you don't like it?

YOU ARE NEVER STUCK WITH YOU

Your golfing past may be compelling, but it is not an unyielding dictator. If you don't like your outcomes, you can change your response patterns, if you want to. You are never stuck with you unless you choose to be.

The first step in changing is to stop immortalizing the memory of your golf failures—Tracks of Failure—and start replacing them with powerful neural networks of success—Tracks of Excellence. You can do this by selectively emotionalizing your positive experiences as you play, and treating the negative experiences with just enough disdain to make them useful. As Chuck Hogan has showed us, most golfers overemotionalize their bad shots and underemotionalize the good ones, and I am suggesting that you simply reverse the process—heavily mark the good shots and lightly mark the bad. You want to remember the bad shots, but only as information for your Strength and Weakness Profile. *Bad shots are saved as guidelines that will make you a better player; good shots are saved as proof that you can be a good player.*

TRUE LIES

One of the reasons why lie detector tests are not admissible in court is that people must know they are lying for detection to occur. But there are many examples of people who are not telling the truth, but don't know they are lying. One example is Edward Daily, who was remembered for his bravery in Korea until an investigation by the Associated Press showed that his record was not as he portrayed it. Daily had written a book and organized a veterans' reunion for his regiment at which he recounted stories of his exploits to soldiers who had actually been there.

But Daily was the agent for his own undoing as he agreed to help the Associated Press investigate a war atrocity that occurred at No Gun Ri. He gave them the names of the soldiers to call to verify his role and even confessed to taking part in the killing of defenseless civilians, even though he was not there at the time. After telling the stories for so long, Daily had begun to believe them. He had inserted himself into the events not only in the minds of others but in his own mind as well. He had changed his own personal history.

THE ROLE OF EMOTIONS

Guilt, and Everything Else, by Association

In his book *Descartes' Error,* Antonio Damasio, MD, PhD, argues that, instead of being irrational responses that cloud our judgment, emotions are actually a valuable marking system that allows us to immediately evaluate and respond to an event based on similar events that occurred in the past. Emotions are augments to our reason and, therefore, an important tool for survival. Emotions can tell us what situations to move toward, and what situations to avoid, without going through a time-consuming chain of if-then reasoning.

When a situation presents itself, it inherits an emotional tag by virtue of its association with similar past events that have already been marked: bad-by-association generates "move away from," whereas good-by-association promotes "move toward." The beauty of this avoid-embrace continuum is that you can move along it as rapidly as the situation changes. Logic is a powerful digital tool but in certain situations that call for immediate and accurate responses, logic uses up valuable time that is better spent either fighting or fleeing.

Emotions then are analog markers that even the most verbal have difficulty describing in words. When you "have" an emotion you know intuitively what it is and how to act, but if you haven't had a particular emotion, no amount of description will help you fully comprehend it. Young girls often ask their mothers, "What does it feel like when you fall in love? How will I know?" And the wise mother answers, "Don't worry, you'll know!"

Where Do Emotions Come From?

To understand why our emotions sometimes run wild on the golf course, consider the origins of emotions. Undoubtedly, the first emotions to emerge in humans were directly related to survival. Our modern behavior, although softened and more humane, is nevertheless influenced by mechanisms developed to solve two major primal issues—survival and reproduction. So a prehistoric encounter sorted itself out in one of two ways—kill or mate.

Brutal stuff, to be sure, but according to recent scientific findings, most people have intense fantasies that are residues of these primal emotions. Dr. Peter R. Crabb, an associate professor of psychology at Pennsylvania State University's Abington campus, says that many people fantasize about murder in graphic detail. He goes on to say that "homicidal fantasies may be a relatively normal phenomenon with roots in the evolutionary history of the species."

We appear to have memories tucked away in our DNA that

are triggered by modern-day mock threats. Golf, for instance, with all its challenges and threats, can be a major-league emotional experience. Paul Azinger said that under the pressure of high-stakes Tour golf, "you can feel your pulse in your eyeballs." And it's not just Tour professionals. It is not unusual for any golfer going into competition to be scared, nerves on edge, heart pounding, and palms sweating. Why is this if it's just a game?

Tests of Fear

Part of it has to do with the fact that built into our brains is a hardwired survival system that, when triggered by threat and fear, releases a cascade of powerful, sometimes euphoric chemicals. For survival, it's very handy to be scared of things like mastodons and poisonous snakes. Today, we no longer battle for our lives on a daily basis as we did thousands of years ago, but we still have that elegant alarm system. Rather than let it go to waste, we feed it with manufactured threats that allow us to vicariously take "tests of fear" in a safe environment. Multibillion-dollar industries are devoted to tweak our alarm system: theme parks with roller coaster rides, Steven King novels, horror movies, and professional sports are designed to get our juices flowing.

Why? To use the hardwiring we already have in place evokes a pleasure as palpable as exercising our muscles. We can't have all this sophisticated machinery and not use it; that would be like taking your Ferrari out only to the grocery store. Fear and anger are part of us, and we spend a lot of time and effort devising situations that will rev up the machinery so we can take it for a safe spin around the track—and golf is one of them.

This is all well and good but, as noted in Chapter 5, you must be careful to keep this reaction under control, with the help of the relaxation response, if necessary, or it will flood you with antigolf chemicals and ruin your game.

EMOTIONAL INTELLIGENCE

In his book *Emotional Intelligence*, Daniel Goleman outlines the effects of emotions on memories: "The more intense the arousal, the stronger the imprint; the experiences that scare or thrill us the most in life are among our most indelible memories. This means that, in effect, the brain has two memory systems, one for ordinary facts (System I) and one for Emotionally charged experiences (System II)."

That's why, if you're old enough, you probably remember exactly where you were when John F. Kennedy was assassinated. And if you love golf, it's hard to forget Tiger Woods's domination of the field at the 2000 U.S. Open, Jack Nicklaus's twentieth Majors Championship victory in the 1986 Masters, or Arnold Palmer's emotional wave good-bye to the golf world as he crossed the footbridge on the 18th hole at St. Andrews in his final British Open appearance. These neural footprints are made indelible and instantly available for recall because of the heavyweight emotions you have attached to them.

WHERE WERE YOU IN '63?
On November 22, 1963, President John F. Kennedy was assassinated in Dallas, Texas. I can remember exactly where I was when I heard the news on my car radio. I was about to drive through a highway underpass in Newton, Massachusetts. I remember everything about that moment—I was in a red Ford convertible, a recent graduation present; the sun was shining brilliantly, and I could see the graffiti on the sides of the underpass. Why would I so vividly remember what happened in 1963 when I can't remember what happened last week unless I check my planner? The answer is that, regardless of whether you were a Republican or Democrat, the assassination was a highly charged emotional experience for the

entire country. I marked this event with heavy emotion and, as a result, it's indelibly etched in the upper-level hierarchy of my memory.

How to Use the Marker

Knowing the role emotions play in storing and recalling memories allows you to build a successful golf database. The more times you emotionalize an event, the faster and more vividly you'll remember it; therefore, you'll want to be careful how you react to your experiences on the golf course. To run your own brain effectively and control your emotions, first recognize that they are *your* emotions and, with some practice, you can use them to mark events as it serves you.

A ROUND WITH BOB

Let's play a few holes with Bob to see how emotions can affect a golf game. Bob hits a big slice off the 1st tee that goes out of bounds, and before the ball even lands, he starts swearing and pounding his club on the ground in anger. Bob may not realize it, but his behavior has made the situation much worse than if he just took the simple stroke and distance penalty added to his score. Thanks to his angry reaction, this small piece of his experience that lasted only a few seconds is immortalized in his brain. He's created a deep, Sasquatch-like neural footprint, a memory Track of Failure that will serve to influence not only his current behavior but also his future performance. While one incident may not be fatal, if this behavior becomes a habit—that is, if Bob reacts with intense bursts of anger and frustration for each bad shot—the cumulative effect will be so heavy it will drag his game down to the depths.

Some People Just Can't Accept a Compliment

Now we skip to the 5th hole, where Bob has finally hit a drive in the middle of the fairway. He popped it up just a little bit but it's okay and you say, "Nice shot, Bob." He says, vehemently, "No, that was no good. I hit it too high on the club face. I didn't hit that well at all." For four holes, he needed a scout and a compass to find his tee shots, and finally he hits it in play, in a decent position, and he finds something wrong with it. Granted, the shot was not emotionalized as heavily as the out-of-bounds incident, but it still laid down a Track of Failure that will be part of his memory recall next time he encounters a similar situation. Next time his Track of Failure will have input into the quality of the shot he'll hit.

That's Why They Call Me Bob

Now we're at the 12th hole, where, finally, everything comes together and Bob hits it right in the center of the club face, driving it about 270 yards down the middle of the fairway. Now you're sure it's safe to compliment him, so you say, "Nice shot, Bob." And in a detached, matter-of-fact tone, he says, "Yeah, well, that's what all the practice is about; that's why they put the name on the bag. *That's* why they call me Bob."

Now Bob may not actually say all that but, internally, that's how he emotionalized the dead-center 270-yard drive. This flat response lays down a weak, birdlike neural footprint that's stored as a System I event, a noncompelling piece of information filed at the bottom of the hierarchy. At this rate, if Bob played for eighteen holes (or for eighteen years) using this marking pattern, all of his high-level memories would be Tracks of Failure and there is no way you can play to your talent level (amateur or professional) saddled with such a besmirched database. You may play good golf, but it isn't the best golf *you* can play.

Can He Switch It? Can You?

What would compel Bob to emotionalize everything bad that happened to him and neutralize everything good that came his way? Why would he associate intimately with the bad and dissociate from the good? One reason is that this type of response had become a habit and another reason is that he doesn't realize he's doing it—which is why his response patterns have become habitual. Is there any way Bob can turn this around so he can dissociate from the bad and associate with the good? Can he run his own brain?

If He Has a Mind To

Yes, Bob can run his own brain, and so can you, but first he has to realize that he's creating Tracks of Failure, and then he has to change his behavior. Bob doesn't have to continue to do it the way he did it in the past. He could turn it all around *if he has a mind to.*

Others Run Their Brain

The ability to control the mind has been well documented in science. By learning to control their respiration, Indian yogis have survived long periods in an environment with an oxygen level so low (such as being buried alive) that it would kill the average person. There are films of Buddhist monks drying soaking-wet sheets in 40-degree temperatures by wrapping them around their naked bodies. Within five minutes, the sheets begin to steam as the monks, using the power of their mind, elevate their temperatures and turn their bodies into clothes dryers.

Another proof that learning to control your thoughts and emotions is a powerful tool for change is a study by UCLA professor Dr. Jeffrey Schwarz, who observed that when obsessive-compulsive patients changed the way they *thought* about a situation, they literally changed their brain's hardwiring. In other words, mind can change matter.

Now, if monks can dry sheets with their mental control, and obsessive-compulsive patients can be taught to change the way their brains are wired to help their illness, then certainly you can teach yourself to transform your Tracks of Failure into Tracks of Excellence in order to play better golf. Let's see how Bob could turn it around, if he decided to run his brain the way he should.

The Turnaround

When Bob finally hit that perfect drive off the 12th tee, he could have marked it as high-priority by emotionalizing it, creating a deep Track of Excellence. He could have gotten excited about it, enough to let his brain know that this kind of experience bears repeating. And when he hit a pop-up off the 5th tee, he could have found something good about it and then emotionalized that. He could have thought, "Well, now, that's better, things are turning around," a response pattern that would have laid down a Track of Excellence rather than a Track of Failure.

A turnaround from negative to positive, where you mark a peak golf experience, isn't hard to do. Neither is finding some good in a mediocre outcome. Those are easy habits to adopt; the hard part is handling the bad shot. What is Bob to do about the first swing of the day—the slice out of bounds?

The ultimate reaction would be to dissociate completely from the event by treating it as a System I event; after all, it's just a piece of experience and it's only golf. There are far more important things—like good health and family. And, if Bob was able to detach himself from his good shot, why can't he switch that around and detach himself from the bad shot? Well, there is the matter of being human.

The Substitution

To Bob, as to many who love golf, failure is upsetting—very upsetting to some, and less for others. Bob will always express his frustration and be disappointed with his bad shots, but he needs to stay away from anger and fury. Marking the event as something to avoid is natural, but marking it with nuclear intensity is detrimental to his game. On a scale that ranges from tepid to rabid, his response can be negative but it needs to be cooler.

Repetition and intensity are the two elements involved in depositing a memory track. If one is absent, the other's effect is somewhat weakened. There have been many players who have a history of getting upset when they play. Craig Stadler lets you know he cares; Curtis Strange has muttered some oaths; Steve Pate is known as the Volcano; Colin Montgomery regularly turns beet red when things don't go his way. Even the phenomenal Tiger Woods has been known to call himself names and get upset when he hits a bad shot, but he also leads the Tour in a statistic called "bounce back," which is the ability to make birdie or better after you've just made bogey or worse on the previous hole. The difference is, these great players get mad, and then they get over it.

To paraphrase the great Bobby Jones, there are some emotions that you cannot endure with the club still in your hands and, on occasion, most of us have felt the urge to let one fly. Golf's most angry man was probably Guy Laffon, an accomplished player during the early days of the Tour. On one occasion, after missing an important putt, he punched himself so hard he knocked himself out. Another time, on the way to the next tee after a missed putt, he impaled the hand responsible for the yip on the spines of a cactus. With blood spurting from the offending appendage, he was forced to withdraw from the tournament.

A PASSION FOR THE GAME

One of my students, the head of a successful law firm, demonstrated his emotion for the game with passion rather than anger. Fred had a 17 handicap when we met and in six months, with much dedication, his handicap was rapidly approaching single digits. His wife said that one winter night she caught Fred at 11:00 P.M., in his bathrobe, taking swings in the snow to check his swing path. That's dedication. The next summer Fred told me that he was riding his bike down a long grade with no shoulder on the road when he saw in his rearview mirror an eighteen-wheeler bearing down on him. He thought he was a goner and it flashed through his mind, "Please, God, not now when I'm finally getting my swing down."

Now the Freds and Bobs and Tigers of this world are not going to treat an out-of-bounds on the first swing of the day as just a piece of information, but they can make sure that their response is measured so they don't create a deep Track of Failure. The prescription then for the really bad shots is: get annoyed but not volcanic; get disappointed but not crushed; get frustrated but not furious—then be done with it. Think of it this way: if you really care about your game, you need to preserve its long-term health by administering an emotional palliative to the dicey situations where a serious Track of Failure could result. Concern is one thing, fury is quite another. In golf, controlling the ball is critical, but to do so you first have to learn to control yourself. In this regard, your emotional system is not some out-of-control, loose cannon but a valuable resource that can be made to do your bidding. Here's how.

ANCHORS

An anchor is a part of an experience that can be used to bring back the entire experience. It is a piece so representative of the whole experience that when you think of that piece, you automatically recall the entire experience, complete with emotions. It's like a string of pearls—pull on one pearl and you pull up the entire string.

It might be a visual anchor: you see someone from your past

who helps you recall certain events. Class reunions, for example, are full of anchors. It may be a kinesthetic anchor—the strong handshake of a stranger reminds you of your father; an olfactory anchor—the smell of cookies opens the floodgates to childhood reminiscences; a gustatory anchor—the taste of a rum and Coke makes you remember your first hangover; or an auditory anchor—a song brings back the memory of a long-lost love.

In the same way, anchors can help you have permanent access not only to your swing but also to your entire golf game. Once you learn your swing, you don't lose it. The motor program is still in your brain; you're just denied full access to it. Anchors can help you retrieve your swing and with it your ability to play.

Types of Anchors

Anchors have to fit your personality so you are comfortable with them. Therefore, there are as many anchors as there are golfers: Chi Chi Rodriguez's saber dance, Tiger's gliding fist pump, and Palmer hitching his pants are some famous anchors. One of my students wore a rubber band and snapped himself to mark a good shot. Smiling inwardly during the rush of excitement and satisfaction of a good shot, nodding your head and saying, "Yes," high-fives, and using image words like "feathers" or a phrase like "grip it and rip" all are examples of anchors that can be used both before the shot to call up the memory of what you want to do and after the shot to mark your performance.

Choosing an Anchor

Sometimes you choose your anchor and sometimes it's chosen for you. Simply by being part of a social group or culture, you inherit anchors that are an integral part of the fabric of your group. To most Americans, the American flag is a visual anchor that evokes emotions and recalls particular events. For example, the raising of the Stars and Stripes on Iwo Jima is a scene that calls up vivid memories and emotions, especially for World War

II veterans. In the same way, one's national anthem is an equally powerful auditory anchor. In hypnosis, analysts plant anchors in the subject's mind to help them defuse certain types of mental turmoil. The experts on Madison Avenue lob anchors at us using every conceivable medium to keep their products popping into our minds as often as possible.

In a more sinister use, brainwashing techniques similar to those depicted in the 1962 movie classic *The Manchurian Candidate* employ anchors that, once embedded in the brain, can be stimulated months or years later to control the subject's behavior. In *The Manchurian Candidate,* a group of captive American soldiers is being brainwashed by a Chinese Communist hypnotist. One soldier, played by Laurence Harvey, is programmed to return home to America and wait for the anchor (a buried hypnotic suggestion) to be triggered by his controller, an anchor that turns him into an assassin programmed to kill the President of the United States. In this case, the hypnotist used a visual anchor, the queen of diamonds playing card.

One way to use an anchor is to mark events so that you create a Track of Excellence. You hit a good shot, get excited, and anchor it with a unique physical gesture that you reserve only to tag good shots (technique 1 below). The second way to use an anchor is to change a situation in which the outcome is not good (technique 2). The third way is to call up the overall form of your swing with a special form anchor just before you set the club in motion (technique 3). Knowing and using the anchoring techniques is a major skill in running your brain.

Anchoring Technique 1: Marking

The Turnaround Technique
Most people anchor all the time, but, as you saw with Bob, they anchor negatively and stock their databases with bad experiences that confound their game. You can turn this around by

making the technique outlined below an integral part of the evaluation period that occurs at the end of your 30-Second Swing.

1. When you hit a good golf shot, anchor it to create a Track of Excellence that will be stored at the top of the hierarchy in your brain.

2. When you hit a mediocre shot, find something good about it, then anchor it, creating a Track of Excellence that will be stored somewhere in the middle of the hierarchy.

3. When you hit a bad shot, treat it as something you don't want to repeat but as a piece of information for your Strength and Weakness Profile. In this way, you deal with it but you don't embed it as a deep Track of Failure. Mark the bad outcome with a prearranged phrase or gesture such as "That's not what I had in mind" or a shrug of the shoulders or a shake of your head. Chuck Hogan, a pioneer of this technique, suggests the phrase "That's interesting." This way you'll remember your weakness so you can be self-correcting.

The last step is to replay the shot with a practice swing while you create mental images of the outcome you wanted. Make it right in your replay, then use an anchor to create a Track of Excellence. It takes only a few seconds for you to see, feel, and hear the good outcome in your mind—think of it as a mental mulligan. The replay creates a new situation with a new outcome. It does not replace the bad event but it does supersede it in the hierarchy.

Most playing professionals go through this process after the cameras have switched to the next competitor, so you'll rarely see the process on television. Corey Pavin and Gary Player make a replay swing after almost every shot that doesn't produce the result they wanted—and so does Tiger Woods.

Practice this Turnaround Technique at every opportunity. Dedicate entire rounds to doing this: forget about both your score and your swing and focus instead on laying down Tracks of Excellence and avoid mak-

ing Tracks of Failure. You'll be surprised how soon the process becomes an automatic part of your 30-Second Swing.

As an adjunct to your on-course use of anchoring, after you finish playing or practicing, mentally replay all the things you did correctly. If you forgot to anchor something at the time it actually happened, do it during your replay session. Reflect on the good shots you hit and the feelings and states of mind that made your game enjoyable. Keep replaying your mental golf movie until it's burned into your memory.

Anchoring Technique 2: Embedding

Does This Ring a Bell?

In addition to labeling outcomes, another valuable use of anchoring is to change the situation itself by embedding an external anchor into the fabric of the experience. A famous example of the embedding anchor is the Russian scientist Pavlov conditioning dogs to salivate at the sound of a bell. He displayed food to the dogs and then rang a bell as they were salivating. After enough repetitions, all he had to do was ring the bell (an external auditory anchor) and the dogs would salivate although no food was present. Hearing the bell was now part of the situation, the piece that could bring back the whole experience.

BE YOUR OWN PAVLOV

Your Strength and Weakness Profile is not just composed of how good you are with a particular club. It should also contain a profile of situations in your golf game where you excel, as well as situations that give you trouble. Your goal should be to digitize these situations by defining the who-what-where-when-why-how parameters of each, then deal with the situations that need attention, one by one, as outlined below.

An Example

A student of mine had a bad case of the 1st-tee jitters—not the normal nervousness we all have where the butterflies are flying in formation, but a full-blown case of fright in which his butterflies were dive-bombing. It was a tremendous weakness in his game because he would invariably hit a bad shot, getting him into trouble from the get-go. He'd then spend the next few holes trying to recover. Here is how we digitized this part of his situational Strength and Weakness Profile.

Who was involved: It happened every time someone was watching him teeing off the first tee, including his playing partners and especially if there was someone new in the group.

What happened: He hyperventilated, and had a rush of adrenaline so intense that he felt weak-legged and the feel for his swing disappeared. This caused him to hit poor shots early in his round, especially off the 1st tee.

Where/When it happened: On the 1st tee especially, but also whenever someone like a ranger or maintenance worker stopped to watch him as he played.

Why it happened: He's playing What Will People Think of Me? instead of golf.

How anchoring can help: He used the technique of embedding to rectify this situation. I asked him to recall a situation where he was calm and relaxed, the best choice being a repetitive situation rather than a one-time event. The situation he chose occurred most every day of the workweek around 7:00 P.M. when he turned off his telephone and read his daily paper. This was his decompression period, a situation designed to relax him. The anchor we chose to embed was a feel anchor where he pumped his fist by clenching and then relaxing his left hand. He embedded two situations: when he was actually in the situation, and when he imagined he was in the situation. After doing this for about two weeks, he had installed the anchor so that when he pumped his fist, a wave of calm swept over him.

Now with the state of calm linked to the fist pump, he was

ready to embed this link into the 1st tee–jitters experience. His goal was to fire the anchor every time he thought about or actually experienced the 1st-tee situation. In addition, he took a deep breath (as outlined in Chapter 5) to help him relax each time he used his anchor. Since he played only once a week, it took about three months before he saw the reward of his effort. The embedding process takes time, and the improvement is incremental rather than a sudden epiphany. But, as he learned to relax, he hit better and better shots off the 1st tee and he made sure to anchor each good shot. Over time he actually rewired his database so that he eliminated his 1st-tee phobia.

Anchoring Technique 3: Form Anchoring

The third way you can use anchoring is to recall the overall form of your swing just before you set the club in motion. You've learned that what is actually stored in your brain is the form of your swing and that, for each swing, you fill the substance into that form. For example, part of the form is balance, and the substance that fills in the form is the specific movements of leg action and pressure transfer. To set this process in motion, you use an anchor that acts as the link between the form and the substance.

Be aware that you are not limited to one type of anchor. In fact, most good players string anchors together as part of their multisensorial avalanche. Common kinesthetic anchors like waggles or triggers are often linked to auditory anchors, such as "grip it and rip it," and visual anchors, such as images of the target or the shot.

IT'S POWERFUL STUFF

Anchoring is powerful stuff because it fits perfectly with the workings of the human brain. It's no surprise then that anchoring has been used throughout recorded history by anyone interested in running someone else's brain—from pharaohs building pyramids to snake oil salesmen and voodoo priests selling life and death respectively. The good news is that if you know how to run your own brain, you can control this process and put it to work for you, something champions have learned to do.

It has been said that 5 percent of the people in the world control 95 percent of the world's wealth and, if by some magic that wealth were redistributed evenly, the 5 percent would have their wealth back in a relatively short time. There's no way to know if the theory is true, but it makes sense. In all my years of teaching, coaching, and observing people in this regard, only about 5 percent of them run their own brain; the other 95 percent let others run it for them.

SKILL ENHANCEMENT

We all know at least one person (call him or her the Topper) who, no matter which subject you bring up or story you tell, has been there, done that, only better. The exaggerations and lies are an attempt to prop up a weak self-image. The Topper is caught in a life-long game he can never win called "I Can Top That" in which in order to be successful he has to make up stuff. Sometimes it's comical—you're recounting the story of Gene Sarazen's double eagle and the Topper claims to have been there at the 15th hole at Augusta in 1935, no doubt whispering, "Gene, hit the four wood." Sometimes it's unfair—the Topper takes credit for things that other people did. And sometimes it's scary because the Topper tells the story so many times that he actually comes to believe it. How could this happen? How do people airbrush themselves into history? It has to do with how your brain stores and recalls memories. Your brain stores your experiences, but it doesn't recall experiences perfectly, word for word, like an audiotape. The recollection is more like a mosaic, built with bits and pieces that resemble the nuts and bolts of the experience, but are not identical to it.

In order to record your experience, your brain breaks the event down into a number of pieces and sends these pieces to different parts of the brain for storage. The advantage is that you can injure one area of your brain without destroying your entire memory of the experience. All the caveman had to remember was the gross meaning of an event—that tigers are bad and turkeys are good; run from one and run after the other. Today, if you're a tiger-ologist, you need to know a lot more about tigers than the caveman did, but your brain still uses its million-year-old format of multiple storage addresses.

When your memory is triggered, you reassemble the pieces by calling them back together from the various corners of your brain. And here's the key—the exact piece doesn't always show up for the reunion, because there are other similar pieces stored in the same category. Therefore, by remembering an event, you may change it slightly. In some cases, if you do this enough, it can become a memory trace that is different enough to be a new experience with identifiable neural footprints of its own. In essence, the memory is a synthetic self-manufactured experience that is as real to you as if you actually had the experience.

Therefore, in addition to using the Turnaround Technique to lay down Tracks of Excellence while you play, you can actually change the contents of your neural storage bin using a process called Skill-Enhancing Imagery. There are two parts to it: Part 1, eliciting the relaxation response, and Part 2, implanting the Tracks of Excellence.

Part 1: The Relaxation Response

Herbert Benson, MD, a leading heart specialist from Harvard, conducted extensive research into how the relaxation response works and concluded that it is pivotal for changing behavioral states and certain motor activity states.

Studies show that during meditation both brain hemispheres are in sync, creating a brain state in which capabilities are magnified.

How to Elicit the Relaxation Response

1. Find a quiet place where you won't be disturbed. Sit with your back straight, resting against a support such as a wall. Fold and cross your legs in front of you in the lotus position. It helps if you use earplugs because it's easier to isolate the sound of your breathing, a key element in the exercise.

2. Inhale through your nostrils so that your breath fills your stomach. Once you fill your abdominal cavity, continue your breath and fill your upper chest cavity. This method gives you a full exchange that reoxygenates your blood and expels harmful carbon dioxide.

3. Once you've inhaled using this low to high technique (first abdominal, then thoracic), use your stomach muscles to expel the air through your mouth. Place your hand on your abdomen to feel it swell as you breathe in and contract as you breathe out. Once you find a rhythm, relax and focus on the sound of your breathing to the exclusion of all else.

4. Continue as in steps two and three until you're in a complete state of relaxation. At first, it might take you fifteen minutes or more to elicit the relaxation response, but as you become more adept, you can do it in less than a minute.

"In this 'tis a microcosm of the world's larger discipline. Our feelings, fantasies, thoughts and muscles all must join the

> play. In golf, you see the essence of what the world itself demands. Inclusion of all our parts, alignment of them all with one another and with the clubs and with the ball with all the land we play on and with our playing partners. The game requires us to join ourselves to the weather, to notice subtle energies that change each day upon the links and the subtle feelings of those around us. It rewards us when we bring them all together, our bodies and our minds, our feelings and our fantasies—rewards us when we do and treats us badly when we don't. The game is a mighty teacher."
>
> —Michael Murphy, *Golf in the Kingdom*

Part 2: Implanting Tracks of Excellence

CNS Can't Tell

The fact that the central nervous system (the brain and the spinal cord) cannot tell the difference between a perfectly imagined event and a real one is documented both in the laboratory and in certain everyday experiences. For example, in the shower, with a relaxing cascade of hot water on your back, it's easy to go into a state of reverie where images are so compelling that you are transported to some other place and time. If your brain waves could be measured, they would show that you are having a multisensorial, perfectly imagined illusion. It is the same in the half-awake/half-asleep state just before you wake up from a dream. For a split second, you are certain the dream was real.

Eastern European coaches pioneered the technique of training their athletes to image their performance before their competitions. For example, a slalom skier, under the influence of the relaxation response, would ski the course in his mind. Using electrodes attached to the surface of the athlete's skin, muscular contractions were recorded. The results showed that the athlete was using 90 percent of the muscles in his perfectly imagined ski run that he would have used if he had been skiing for real. In effect, the central nervous system could not tell the difference between the real and the perfectly imagined.

Many studies have shown that images perfectly pictured in the mind are thought of as real to your subconscious. As Hutchison explains, "Visualizing yourself skillfully performing some action can be as effective as actually performing the action; mental images produce real physical and mental effects. The problem is that most of us find it hard to visualize with the kind of total concentration and clarity necessary to convince our body it's actually happening."

So the second step, once you're relaxed, is to visualize the part of your golf game you want to improve. Select one element of your mechanics that needs work—your grip or your swing path or something more global like your Time IQ or your balance—and imagine yourself performing the move perfectly. Drape your recall with as much sense data as you can muster, so that you see it, hear it, smell it, and feel it in natural colors and real time. At first, your images will be fleeting and washed out but, after a week or two, you'll be able to make them lifelike, and then things start to happen.

SELL YOURSELF

While you are under the auspices of imagery, sell yourself on the particular "product" you want to acquire. Salespeople know the worth of the fact-benefit-close sequence and it can help you buy into your swing changes. First, state the facts about say the grip change you need to make, for example: "I can't play well without a grip that matches the rest of my swing." Next, tell yourself how the change will help: "I leave too many balls to the right and a stronger grip will help me square the club face at impact." Finally, don't forget to close the deal by seeing-feeling-hearing yourself using the new grip.

Or let's say you need practice hitting your driver. Imagine yourself addressing the ball, then your solid stance, your graceful backswing, the controlled power of your downswing, pure contact, the streaking ball flight, and finally the ball landing on your target. The more precise you make your image, the more effective your mental practice. With absolute clarity, you view the scene in all its precision without any fuzzy edges. You focus in as if you were watching it through a telescopic lens, and then you zoom back out and see the whole scene. You see how you're dressed, you see the colors, and you see the size of the ball, the name on the ball, the club head. And, most important, you feel what it feels like to be you.

SYNTHETIC GOLF MEMORIES: CHANGING YOUR TRACKS OF FAILURE

Good Lies: The Older I Get, the Better I Used to Play

A high percentage of research subjects fed false details about their childhood can be convinced that certain things happened to them, even though they didn't. Dr. Henry Roediger of Washington University in St. Louis and other researchers have documented the human willingness to recall things that make sense, that might have or should have happened, but didn't. The brains of these subjects have physically changed and once the ersatz memories are installed, as with the Topper I described earlier, the subjects can't tell the difference between the real and the false. The research proves that there is a biology of false memories, and if you know how it works you can use it to your advantage to create good lies for a better golf game.

Not only can you ingrain Tracks of Excellence, as outlined above, but you can also convert your Tracks of Failure to Tracks of Excellence. If you implant the false memory of the good shot correctly, it will become real to you. In other words, you can be a historical revisionist by seeding your brain with memories of good shots even though you didn't actually hit them. It's best to do this with shots you have the ability to hit but failed to pull off in a situation, or else your brain won't buy it. It's not helpful to imagine a 300-yard drive if you simply can't hit one.

You might imagine a particular shot, like a driver that you hit out of bounds, or a pressure putt you missed. Then choose one resource that you would have needed during that experience in order to have a good outcome. It might be that you tried to hit your driver too hard and the resource you needed to add to the mix was less force and better timing. Whatever it is that you need to add to the recall to make it a Track of Excellence, identify it and then insert it in the image process.

If you don't have the necessary resources in your current Strength and Weakness Profile, make it your priority to acquire those resources. If you always slice your driver, take a lesson; not a general swing lesson but a "resource acquisition" lesson dedicated to curing your driver slice. If you're nervous, practice your breathing until you can control the anxiety. If you institute a program of specific resource acquisition for each weakness, soon you will have a powerful repertoire with which to image.

This mental control that I have described isn't just pie-in-the-sky—it works. Using brain scans, studies at the Institute of Neurology in London prove that when you image an event like your golf swing, the mental picture turns on most of the brain networks used for a real swing. And the more you do this imaging, the stronger the neural footprints become. Since your central nervous system can't tell the difference between a perfectly imagined event and a real one, the better you are at creating life-like images of good shots, the easier it is to implant them as real.

BOOK SUMMARY

Is it the swing that makes a champion? There are really two answers to this: yes, in that the swing itself is a vehicle that gets champions to the first tee, and no, in that there is far more to the game than simply making a physical swing. As I have said, if the swing is the thing, then a champion could be chosen simply by watching the field of players hit balls with a judge rating them for the quality of their swings, much as a judge decides who the best skater is or which dog is best of show. But, of course, as Sam Snead so aptly put it, "The sun don't shine on the same dog every day," which is why, regardless of pedigree or past performance, you still have to play the game to determine the champion.

Anyone who is familiar with journeyman Ed Fiori's victory over Tiger Woods, Paul Runyan's win against Sam Snead, or John Daly's besting a field of sweet swingers in two major championships knows that there is so much more to golf than the swing. And that so much more is what this book has examined in its attempt to characterize the difference between a golfer and a champion. Champions have learned a secret that not a lot of golfers ever learn: once you've got a repeatable swing, it's how you train and then run your brain that decides how good you'll be. This book has offered you techniques for developing the "Traits of the Greats" that will allow you to play to your potential, to be your own personal champion.

Traits of the Great That Will Make You Your Own Personal Champion

Great players have control of their STAR and can turn it on a moment's notice so that their responses are always perfectly fit to the exigencies of the situation. This fluidity allows them lightning reaction time so they can lead with their strengths, thereby maximizing their minute-by-minute performance. This is the antithesis of a fixed and stultifying personality type who has a low adaptability profile.

Great players have an accurate Strength and Weakness Profile, an accurate assessment of their ability to play every shot in the game. Based on this profile, they play the game by fitting their current Strength and Weakness Profile into the defenses set up by the architect, taking into consideration the conditions (wind, lie, distance, etc.) and the circumstances of play (match or medal).

Great players understand that golf is a target game. They don't play "golf swing," and they don't play "golf shot"; they play "target golf." And to do this, they have a number of techniques that allow them to make the target loom on their mental screen.

Great players don't play by "do's" and they don't play by "don'ts." They create a target/player bonding for every shot and they stay in the loop by maintaining their total commitment to the shot they have chosen to play.

Great players train and then manage their brain while they play, keeping their external tracking systems (visual, auditory, kinesthetic) open and unclogged so they can lock onto the target like a heat-seeking missile.

Great players are in the right mode at the right time. They match the mode they are in to the demands of the situation—the analytical mode when they need a plan, the physical mode when they need to make a good swing, and the emotional mode when they respond to the outcome of their effort.

Great players honor their No signals and are empowered by their Go signals. They have learned the invaluable technique of turning No signals into Go signals and so they play in a constant flow of Go signals known as the Zone.

Great players create Tracks of Excellence (TOEs) rather than Tracks of Failure, and their TOEs provide a positive golfing database that they draw on while they play.

I have tried to shed some light on what's going on in that behemoth we call the human brain when we play the game of golf. As Socrates might have said, had he been a golfer, "An unexamined golf game is not worth having." So here's the recipe for success: Put your game under a close and honest examination, use the 30-Second Swing to help you train your brain, throw in a handful of old-fashioned hard work and perseverance, and let it simmer for about thirty or forty rounds of golf. Once your incubation period is satisfied, you'll be primed to play at the highest level possible given your talent for the game—and then what a wonderful time you will have.

The 30-Second Swing
One of the basic techniques you use to run your brain on the golf course. The process by which you organize your experience as you play the game.

Anchor
A piece of an experience so representative of the experience that when you think of that piece, you automatically recall the entire experience, complete with emotions.

Anchoring
The process of marking and embedding experience in the neural networks by using emotions. The more you emotionalize an event, the more influential it becomes in effecting subsequent similar behavior in similar circumstances.

APE
An acronym for the three mind states—analytic, physical, and emotional. As you move through your 30-Second Swing, you'll need to be in the right mode at the right time.

The Bonehead Effect
Strange things that happen when you're under stress and logic and rational thinking take a vacation.

Catalog of Best Shots
A mental list of your all-time best shots for each club that helps you image the shot you have chosen to play.

The Commitment Line
An imaginary line drawn perpendicular to the target line between you and the ball that you don't cross unless you are 100 percent committed to the shot you are about to play.

Controlling the Loom
A major-league strategy for running your brain that involves controlling your mental screen where images of your world are represented.

Cumulative Disreward (CD)
As your round progresses, you make a bunch of good swings but nothing works out, and at some point, because your best efforts go unrewarded, your game collapses.

Embedding
Technique of changing the situation itself by embedding an external anchor into the fabric of the experience.

The Evaluation Phase
The part of the 30-Second Swing where outcomes are evaluated, marked, and then stored as part of an ever-expanding

database that is the source of your up-to-date Strength and Weakness profile.

The Fight/Flight Response
The brain responds to threat by producing antigolf chemicals that flood your body and make it impossible to play your best golf.

Form
The form is universal, while the substance is the particular expression of that form. What your brain stores is the form of your swing, and then with each swing the substance—the actual movements—flows into the form.

Form Anchoring
A technique where you use an anchor to recall the overall form of your swing just before you set the club in motion.

The Four-Target System
A procedure that pinpoints your target by using a four-point reference system that takes advantage of the way your eyes naturally gauge distance and direction.

Foveal Fix
Foveal vision is "straight ahead" vision, the most accurate way to locate the target.

Full Commitment
You make a covenant with yourself (a promise that you will not deviate from the plan) and, in doing so, you consign all your resources to the task at hand.

Golf Balance
The contorted arrangements (tilted spine, bowed body, left side straight, right side flexed, head back, front hip ahead, etc.) involved in hitting a golf ball.

Image Retention Ability (IRA)
A skill that allows you to maintain your visual lock on the target even when you're not looking directly at it.

Internal Messages
Your subconscious communicates in signals and, to play your best golf, you must recognize what these signals are trying to tell you. You may feel unsure or decisive, uneasy or calm, worried or confident, distressed or relaxed, annoyed or serene. These messages are No and Go signals.

LAWS of the Golf Swing
A book describing how the four dimensions (height, width, depth, and time) relate to a golfer's body type. Each body type fills space differently and thus has its own dominant dimension.

Nega-talk
A destructive, glass-is-half-empty type of talk in which you berate yourself, call yourself names, and do yourself absolutely no good.

Never-Never Land
A checklist of course management "don'ts."

Permission
When the conscious mind says, "Let's do it," and the subconscious says, "I've checked it out—go ahead." The congruence between the two gives you permission.

The Pose
The conclusion of the follow-through where you hold the finish of your swing in perfect balance until the ball lands.

Posi-talk
Self-talk where you put a positive interpretation on events and outcomes.

Prophylactic-talk
Self-talk that protects your self-image by placing the blame for failure on outside agencies not under your control.

PSO On-Course Tracking System
Technique to objectively evaluate each shot you hit based on your plan for the shot (P), your swing (S), and the outcome (O). Using this system you'll know which area of your game needs improvement.

Rehearsal
The practice swing is a kinesthetic cue that can serve as a perfect rehearsal for your actual swing.

Relaxation Response
A scientifically verified bodily process that, when initiated, will allow you to take control of your stress level.

Ringmaster of No/Go Signals
A specific part of the brain where the No/Go system is located—a ringmaster that coordinates all of the acts that combine to make us human. No one knows for sure, but a leading candidate is the frontal lobe.

Rumpelstiltskin Solution
Being able to identify/name what's happening to you is an important step in controlling the situation.

Running Your Brain
Understanding how your brain works and developing techniques, attitudes, and contingency strategies that give you control of its day-to-day operation.

Scoring Golf
A type of golf where you use strategy to produce the lowest score possible.

Spectacular Golf
A type of golf where the object is to hit heroic shots by firing at every flag, pounding driver off every par-4 and par-5, and attacking the course regardless of the consequences or the score.

STAR
An acronym for the four basic response patterns on your behavioral compass: Scripter, Terminator, Analyzer, and Relater. A tool that serves as a starting point for training your brain to adapt to changing golf situations—by changing the direction of your STAR.

Street Balance
Human balance system that, among other things, keeps you safe from falling.

Strength and Weakness Profile
To run your brain at any given time, self-knowledge, in the form of a comprehensive, digitized, personal profile is a necessity.

Targeting
Every shot is a target-player interaction where the player connects to the target through the senses, making the connection a multisensorial experience.

"Thinkering"
A destructive combination of thinking about and then tinkering with your golf swing.

Time IQ
How well you control the time dimension when you play golf.

Tracking Systems
Term used to emphasize the fact that the senses locate objects in space and time. For golf the "big three" are visual, kinesthetic, and auditory, and the visual system reigns supreme.

Tracks of Excellence
Neural networks that contain positive golf experience. The goal is to create as many Tracks of Excellence as you can and to limit the production of Tracks of Failure.

Tracks of Failure
Neural networks that contain negative golf experience.

True Lies
Seeding your brain with memories of good shots even though you didn't actually hit them.

The Turnaround
A technique where you emotionalize the good outcomes, mark the bad as information, and mentally replay the bad to create Tracks of Excellence.

The Zone
An unbroken stretch of personal permissions which promote a flow of Go signals as you move from shot to shot.